Needs So
badly 6-5-2012
Prayers are on
page 46-47-48

D0860134

Mothers Day - 2012
from Dana + Rick

The Tender Words of God

Other Books by Ann Spangler

Daily Secrets of the Christian Life,
Hannah Whitall Smith (compiled by Ann Spangler)

Don't Stop Laughing Now!
compiled by Ann Spangler and Shari MacDonald

He's Been Faithful,
Carol Cymbala with Ann Spangler

Immanuel

Look Who's Laughing!
compiled by Ann Spangler and Shari MacDonald

Men of the Bible,
coauthored with Robert Wolgemuth

Praying the Names of God

Praying the Names of Jesus

She Who Laughs, Lasts!
compiled by Ann Spangler

Women of the Bible,
coauthored with Jean Syswerda

Women of the Bible: 52 Stories for Prayer and Reflection

The Tender Words of God

of God

A DAILY GUIDE

ANN SPANGLER

ZONDERVAN®

ZONDERVAN.com/
AUTHORTRACKER
follow your favorite authors

ZONDERVAN®

The Tender Words of God
Copyright © 2008 by Ann Spangler

This title is also available as a Zondervan ebook. Visit www.zondervan.com/ebooks.

This title is also available in a Zondervan audio edition. Visit www.zondervan.fm.

Requests for information should be addressed to:
Zondervan, *Grand Rapids, Michigan* 49530

Library of Congress Cataloging-in-Publication Data

Spangler, Ann.
    The tender words of God / Ann Spangler.
       p. cm.
    Includes bibliographical references
    ISBN 978-0-310-26716-4 (hardcover, jacketed)
    1. Bible—Terminology. 2. Bible—Language, style. 3. Bible—Devotional use.
    I. Title.
    BS525.S63 2008
    242'.5—dc22
                             2008012016

Interior design by Sherri L. Hoffman

Printed in the United States of America

08 09 10 11 12 13 14 • 20 19 18 17 16 15 14 13 12 11 10 9 8 7 6 5 4 3 2 1

As the rain and the snow
    Come down from heaven,
and do not return to it
    without watering the earth
and making it bud and flourish,
    so that it yields seed for the sower
    and bread for the eater,
so is my word that goes out from my mouth:
    It will not return to me empty,
but will accomplish what I desire
    and achieve the purpose for which I sent it.

Isaiah 55:10–11

Contents

A Note to the Reader

While some of the passages included in this book are rendered in first person, as though God is speaking directly to us, others are rendered in third person. Regardless of how God's word was originally recorded, I believe that the Bible is God speaking to us in a unique way. His words are tender and comforting—but not always. As frequently, they are abrasive and startling, aiming, as they do, to bring us back from the precipice where sin leads, to a place of safety and transformation. Whatever the tone of God's Word, I believe his aim is always to speak in a way that enables us to be drawn into relationship with himself.

In this book I have chosen to focus on the tender words of God, to listen with fresh ears to the message of his love—a message that transcends centuries and cultures. Each chapter begins with a brief note describing the primary meaning of the word that forms the focus of the chapter. Some of the Scripture passages chosen for the daily readings will contain the word itself. Other passages are included because they convey the essence of the word without using it.

I hope that you will begin each chapter by reading about the primary meaning of the word. Then, after reading about my response to the word, I hope you will spend a full week—both morning and evening—savoring the Scriptures provided so that you can interact with God's Word. In an effort to help you retain God's tender words, I have included a section at the end of each week entitled "I Will Remember This." This section contains brief passages drawn from the previous seven days. My intention in doing this is to give you something to take with you, offering you the chance to consolidate God's Word in your heart, perhaps by reading these passages more than once, reading them first silently and then out loud, writing them out, or by committing one or more to memory.

In rare instances I have chosen to adapt a particular Scripture passage that might otherwise require historical background to draw out its precise meaning. Wherever this was done, I took care to alter the text as little as possible. For instance, instead of rendering Hosea 11:8–9 as:

"How can I give you up, Ephraim?
    How can I hand you over, Israel?
How can I treat you like Admah?
    How can I make you like Zeboiim?
My heart is changed within me;
    all my compassion is aroused."

I have rendered it:

"How can I give you up?
    How can I hand you over?...
My heart is changed within me;
    all my compassion is aroused."

For a more nuanced understanding of these and other texts included in *The Tender Words of God*, readers may want to read the text of the Bible itself.

As always, I am grateful to associate publisher and executive editor Sandy VanderZicht for her patience, encouragement, flexibility, and editorial insight. All are invaluable to an author, and I am grateful to have benefited from Sandy's wise advice over the course of many years. Thanks also to Verlyn Verbrugge, Zondervan's senior editor at large, for his careful editing of the manuscript. I count myself fortunate to have an editor with a sound knowledge of the biblical languages. Because even the best-edited book might not fare well without effective marketing, special thanks go to Marcy Schorsch for her efforts at getting the word out about this one. My thanks would be incomplete were I to overlook the considerable efforts of my agent, Linda Kenney, whose publishing acumen and unflagging support for me and for this book have greatly advanced the project.

1

The Tender Words

I have never found it easy to believe in God's love for me, except perhaps in the first days and weeks of my conversion. No matter where I turned in those bright days I found evidence of God's gracious care and steady forgiveness. The stern-browed god of my youth had suddenly and unexpectedly receded, and in his place came Jesus, bearing gifts of love and peace. Nearly every prayer in those days was answered, sometimes wondrously. I remember thinking that the problem with many people was that they expected so little from a God who was prepared to give so much.

But years passed and something happened. It wasn't one thing but many. Large things and small things—life ebbing and flowing. It was tests of faith, sometimes passed and sometimes not. It was sins accruing. It was spiritual skirmishes and full-out battles. It was disappointments and difficulties and circumstances beyond comprehending. All these heaped together like a great black mound, casting a shadow over my sense that God still loved me, still cared for me as tenderly as when he had first wooed me and won my heart. Instead of a loved and cherished child of God awash in the sea of God's love, I felt more like a boat whose barnacle-encrusted hull had sat too long in the water. That boat needed to be hoisted out of the salty sea to rest for a time in the sunshine. It needed loving, patient hands to sand through all the layers of sediment down to the bare, smooth boards. It needed fresh protective paint so that it could once again be launched into the shining sea.

But if that was my need, how could I, a rapidly aging single mother of two young children, ever find time to rest and to be restored? My older daughter had recently reminded me that my next birthday was cause for special celebration because on that day my age would exactly match the number of electoral votes possessed by the state of California. If you don't know how many that is, I'm not about to tell you. Suffice it to say they have the most of any state in the union.

Then I had an idea that had little to do with changing my routines but everything to do with changing my focus. It occurred to me after talking with a friend who spoke of a time in her life when she finally became convinced of God's love for her. I expected my friend to reveal something complicated and difficult, some tragedy, perhaps, that God had spared her from. Or maybe she had practiced some hard-fought spiritual discipline that yielded a favorable result. But it was something much simpler. Joan told me that she had merely made a decision—to set aside one month in which to act as though God loved her. Whenever she was tempted to doubt his love, she simply shifted her thoughts and then put the full force of her mind behind believing that God loved her. And that settled it for her—for good.

Joan's confidence in being loved has probably shaped her life in ways that even she does not understand. Recently she saw evidence that it had spilled over into the life of someone close to her when one of her sons during a particularly trying time in his life remarked: "I am so thankful God loves me."

My daughters are ten and twelve, while I am, as they repeatedly point out, rapidly approaching the age of extinction. Maybe that's why I find myself thinking lately about how to provide a secure foundation for them. Perhaps I could buy them each a house, I think. That would at least give them something to fall back on in hard times. But then I remember their college savings accounts, still spare, almost anorexic. I remember also that there are limits to what a parent — to what this parent — can do for her children. But what if I could leave them something better than a fat bank account? Jesus talked about the abundance of his provision when he spoke of the grace God wants to pour into our laps: "a good measure, pressed down, shaken together and running over." I wanted to know God's love in that lavish, pressed down, shaken together and running over kind of way so that I could love more fiercely and faithfully. I wanted there to be a spillover effect in the lives of my daughters.

So I was doubly motivated, determined to receive the grace I was sure God wanted to give so that I could both enjoy and communicate it. But I doubted that merely trying to retrain my thoughts would be enough. I needed something positive to focus my thoughts. Then I remembered the promise that Scripture makes about itself: "For the word of God is living and active. Sharper than any double-edged sword, it penetrates even to dividing soul and spirit, joints and marrow" (Hebrews 4:12). I wanted God's penetrating word to cut away my unbelief, to lay bare my need. I wanted to hear the truth from God's own mouth.

Over the years, I have read through the Bible several times, plowing straight through from Genesis to Revelation, not even skipping those endless genealogies. But like many people who tend to be self-critical, I find it easier to absorb the harsher sounding passages in the Bible than those that speak of God's compassion. Somehow, the tender words seem to roll right off me, much like water that beads up and rolls off a well-waxed automobile.

What would happen, I wondered, if I read through Scripture, this time hunting for the words that every human longs to hear — words of mercy, compassion, peace, and love? Yes, I know that every word of God is to be cherished but what if, for a brief time, I focused only on God's most tender words?

Because I am not the same quick study my friend Joan is, I decided to develop a remedial course for myself in which I could reflect morning and evening on the most tender words of God I could find in the Old and New Testament. Once I had gathered these passages, I wanted to sit with them not just for a few days but for three months. I wanted these words to be like guardians at each end of my day, passages I could soak in and call to mind when I was tempted to disbelieve.

The Tender Words of God is the result of this process. While the core of the book is Scripture, each week is introduced with a few words regarding my progress (or regress) on the journey. Though my remarks are brief, they are intended to chronicle my struggles and joys, not because my quest is all that remarkable but precisely because it is so ordinary, expressing the longing we all have to love and to be loved, especially by the One who made us. I hope you will join me on this journey, soaking in these Scriptures morning and evening, listening for God's voice, and experiencing his presence. You may even want to chronicle the story of your own progress by keeping a journal record of the way God communicates his love to you in this time. God has many things for us to do in this life, but I am convinced that you and I will do them better, with far more joy and greater impact, if we do them with a settled confidence in God's love.

2

God Speaks Words of Compassion

רָחַם

RAHAM

The Hebrew word *raham*, which means "compassion," is intimately connected to the Hebrew word *rehem*, which means "womb." Throughout the Scriptures, God reveals a kind of motherly compassion for his people. In one of the Bible's most moving passages, God reveals himself to Moses as "The LORD, the LORD, the compassionate and gracious God, slow to anger, abounding in love and faithfulness" (Exodus 34:6).

Jesus, too, displays great compassion for those who are needy. In fact, his compassion moves him to act on behalf of the sick, the blind, the hungry, and those without a shepherd. He even raises a man from the dead after witnessing a mother's sorrow. Compassion is an attribute of God, and it is closely related to mercy or pity. The Greek New Testament words for compassion are *eleos* and *splanchnon*.

LETTING THE WORD SHAPE ME

I began my hunt for the tender words of God in a distracted state. I was distressed about a deteriorating situation at one of my children's schools. I was thinking about money I didn't have but thought I needed. I felt anxious about a looming deadline. These and other thoughts paraded across my mind—over and over because I hadn't found a way to lay them to rest.

How could I construct a remedial course on God's love when I felt so scattered, when my energy kept heading in other directions? I imagined myself plowing through a field of tall weeds, searching vainly for golden kernels of grain in the midst of a thicket of distractions. But as I began to read the words of Scripture, I felt myself calming down, focusing, resting in the words themselves:

The LORD longs to be gracious to you.

Our God is full of compassion.

In all their distress he too was distressed.

God lifted them up and carried them all the days of old.

And the LORD said, "I will cause all my goodness to pass in front of you."

I imagined Moses encountering the surprise of his life in the desert—a God shocking not so much for the display of his power but for the degree of his love and the intensity of his desire to be known. I listened as the psalmist likened God to a compassionate father and as Isaiah compared the Lord to a mother whose child feeds contentedly at her breast. But what hit me hardest was a story I had heard before, many times. Jesus told it. It's about a son who takes his father's money and runs with it to forlorn places. He lives wildly until the last penny is gone, and then in desperation he hires himself out to feed pigs. Starving, the prodigal son wishes he could stuff his belly with the same food the pigs are eating.

I imagined the listening crowd, captivated by the woeful tale Jesus was telling. The foolish prodigal seems to be getting what he deserves. What a rotten way to treat your father. Having squandered everything, he becomes impoverished. Even worse, he accepts a job taking care of pigs. To associate so closely and constantly with animals that God declared unclean would be to cross a boundary, alienating yourself from a holy God. The prodigal's downward slide must have seemed entirely fitting.

But Jesus' listeners could not have anticipated the surprise ending. Instead of publicly condemning his son and banishing him from the community as would have been a Jewish father's right, the prodigal's father runs out to meet him when he returns home and then throws a party to celebrate his return.

I thought about who was telling the story—the only human being whose vision of God had never been distorted by sin. Wasn't the Son the best one to tell us what God the Father is like?

I also thought about the prodigal. He was a pleasure seeker. I could relate to him because of my own temptations—too much food, comfortable vacations, dreams of an easy life. But dwelling on such dreams makes your body soft and fat, your soul feeble. As I thought about my own tendencies and failures, I could feel myself sinking into a kind of disgust that seemed to move me further from God. But what about the things I had been reading about his compassion? I refocused on what the Scriptures say about God's attitude toward us. As I did, I began to envision him waiting for me in the midst of my weakness, neither surprised nor repulsed by my sin, but simply waiting for me to come to my senses so he could welcome me home.

As this picture of God came into clearer focus, I wondered how often my distorted thinking about him impedes my progress in the spiritual life. Remember what the prodigal was thinking on his way home: "I will set out and go back to my father and say to him: Father, I have sinned against heaven and against you. I am no longer worthy to be called your son; make me like one of your hired men" (Luke 15:18–19). Ashamed of himself, the son completely misunderstood his father's character. He had no idea what was inside his father's heart. Expecting rejection, he must have been shocked by his father's excited welcome — "bring the best ... bring the fattest ... let's have a feast!" (Luke 15:22–23).

That's what sin does to us. It makes us stupid, especially in relationship to God. We find it impossible to conceive of someone whose responses are so much better than our own. We imagine him merely as a larger, more powerful version of ourselves. So we assign him motives that are beneath him and contrary to his nature.

Come to think of it, by doubting his compassion, I was discounting my own experience as a parent. I had long ago realized that having children takes you straight into the mystery of love. Hadn't I known what it felt like to love a child regardless of her stubborn determination to take the wrong path? How could I forget the joy I felt whenever one of my children admitted she had done something wrong and asked to be forgiven? Why did I think God would be a less generous parent than I was? How could I misconstrue his heart, twist his intentions, be so slow to believe in his kindness? After all, I had been created in his image, not he in mine, so it made sense that any goodness in me was merely a reflection of his greater goodness. I knew that any occasional disappointment in my children didn't threaten the foundation of our relationship. How could it when it was built on my fierce, unconditional love for them? Surely God's love was far stronger and deeper than mine.

As I continued to pray to the God of compassion, I felt my own sense of self-condemnation ebbing. I was able to look at my weaknesses calmly, honestly, and with hope because I knew I was standing in the presence of a Father who loved me. Looking at him made it easier to look at me.

Sunday

1-1-2017

IN THE MORNING

I Long to Be Gracious to You

The LORD longs to be gracious to you;
  he rises to show you compassion.
For the LORD is a God of justice.
  Blessed are all who wait for him!

O people of Zion, who live in Jerusalem, you will weep no more. How gracious he will be when you cry for help! As soon as he hears, he will answer you. Although the LORD gives you the bread of adversity and the water of affliction, your teachers will be hidden no more; with your own eyes you will see them. Whether you turn to the right or to the left, your ears will hear a voice behind you, saying, "This is the way; walk in it."

Lord, you are near even when my heart seems far from you. Open my eyes to your presence. Whether I turn to the left or to the right let me encounter your love.

Isaiah 30:18–21

22

AT NIGHT

I Will Reveal Myself to You

Then Moses said [to the LORD], "Now show me your glory."

And the LORD said, "I will cause all my goodness to pass in front of you, and I will proclaim my name, the LORD, in your presence. I will have mercy on whom I will have mercy, and I will have compassion on whom I will have compassion...."

Then the LORD came down in the cloud and stood there with him and proclaimed his name, the LORD. And he passed in front of Moses, proclaiming, "The LORD, the LORD, the compassionate and gracious God, slow to anger, abounding in love and faithfulness."

I will see the goodness of the LORD
    in the land of the living.

Lord, let your goodness pass in front of me. Help me to see you for who you are and to live my life according to this vision.

Exodus 33:18–19; 34:5–7; Psalm 27:13

23

Monday

IN THE MORNING

I Will Welcome You Back

When he [the prodigal son] came to his senses, he said, "How many of my father's hired men have food to spare, and here I am starving to death! I will set out and go back to my father and say to him: Father, I have sinned against heaven and against you. I am no longer worthy to be called your son; make me like one of your hired men." So he got up and went to his father.

But while he was still a long way off, his father saw him and was filled with compassion for him; he ran to his son, threw his arms around him and kissed him.

In all their distress [the LORD] too was distressed,
and the angel of his presence saved them.
In his love and mercy he redeemed them;
he lifted them up and carried them
all the days of old.

Father, your son Jesus compared you to a broken-hearted man who was filled with compassion toward his foolhardy child. Thank you for revealing your father heart toward me today.

Luke 15:17–20; Isaiah 63:9

AT NIGHT

I Will be Your Father

For as high as the heavens are above the earth,
  so great is his love for those who fear him;
as far as the east is from the west,
  so far has he removed our transgressions from us.
As a father has compassion on his children,
  so the LORD has compassion on those who fear him;
for he knows how we are formed,
  he remembers that we are dust.

Lord, you are not surprised at my weakness. I am insubstantial as the dust beneath my feet. And yet you assure me that I am "beloved dust." Don't let me hide this truth from myself but fill me every day with wonder at the greatness of your love.

Psalm 103:11–14

Tuesday

IN THE MORNING

I Will Not Forget You

Shout for joy, O heavens;
> rejoice, O earth;
> burst into song, O mountains!
For the LORD comforts his people
> and will have compassion on his afflicted ones.
But you said, "The LORD has forsaken me,
> the Lord has forgotten me."
"Can a mother forget the baby at her breast
> and have no compassion on the child she has borne?
Though she may forget,
> I will not forget you!
See, I have engraved you on the palms of my hands;
> your walls are ever before me."

Lord, you are more loving than the most faithful of mothers. Thank you for your promise never to abandon, forsake, or forget me. Hold me close, like a child nursing at her mother's breast.

1 - 3 - 2018

Isaiah 49:13–16

AT NIGHT

I Will Show You My Unfailing Love

For people are not cast off
    by the Lord forever.
Though he brings grief, he will show compassion,
    so great is his unfailing love.
For he does not willingly bring affliction
    or grief to any human being.

"Though the mountains be shaken
    and the hills be removed,
yet my unfailing love for you will not be shaken
    nor my covenant of peace be removed,"
    says the [LORD,] who has compassion on you.

Lord, I want to name your faithfulness, to identify you by the way you treat me. So today I call you, not merely Creator, King, and Lord, but the loving God who has shown me compassion.

Lamentations 3:31–33 (TNIV); Isaiah 54:10

Wednesday

IN THE MORNING

I Will Arise and Have Compassion

You will arise and have compassion on Zion,
>   for it is time to show favor to her;
>   the appointed time has come.
For her stones are dear to your servants;
>   her very dust moves them to pity.
The nations will fear the name of the LORD,
>   all the kings of the earth will revere your glory.
For the LORD will rebuild Zion
>   and appear in his glory.
He will respond to the prayer of the destitute;
>   he will not despise their plea.

Lord, you never despise the destitute. Help me not to be ashamed of my desperate need but let it move me to call out to you with hope. May this be the time to show me your favor!

Psalm 102:13–17

AT NIGHT

I Will Not Give You Up!

I will betroth you to me forever;
> I will betroth you in righteousness and justice,
> in love and compassion.

How can I give you up?
> How can I hand you over?...
My heart is changed within me;
> all my compassion is aroused.
I will not carry out my fierce anger....
For I am God, and not man—
> the Holy One among you.
> I will not come in wrath.

For in you, [Lord,] the fatherless find compassion.

Lord, I thank you for the compassion that restrains your anger and defines your heart. I praise you that you don't think or act like a human being but like a holy God, surprising me by your kindness and encouraging me by your passionate love.

Hosea 2:19; 11:8–9; 14:3

Thursday

IN THE MORNING

I Look with Compassion

The LORD is gracious and righteous;
  our God is full of compassion.
The LORD protects the simplehearted;
  when I was in great need, he saved me.
Be at rest once more, O my soul,
  for the LORD has been good to you.
For you, O LORD, have delivered my soul from death,
  my eyes from tears,
  my feet from stumbling.

The LORD will surely comfort Zion
  and will look with compassion on all her ruins;
he will make her deserts like Eden,
  her wastelands like the garden of the LORD.
Joy and gladness will be found in her,
  thanksgiving and the sound of singing.

God, thank you that I can be at rest because of what you have already done for me. Help me to remember your kindness when I become upset or worried. Let the memory of your goodness shape my expectations about the present and the future.

Psalm 116:5–8; Isaiah 51:3

AT NIGHT

I Will Treat You with Kindness

"The LORD will call you back
as if you were a wife deserted and distressed in spirit —
a wife who married young,
only to be rejected," says your God.
"For a brief moment I abandoned you,
but with deep compassion I will bring you back.
In a surge of anger
I hid my face from you for a moment,
but with everlasting kindness
I will have compassion on you,"
says the LORD your Redeemer.
"To me this is like the days of Noah,
when I swore that the waters of Noah would never
again cover the earth.
So now I have sworn not to be angry with you,
never to rebuke you again."

Lord, you use words like brief and momentary to describe your anger and words like deep and everlasting to describe your kindness and compassion. Please don't hide your face from me tonight. Fill me instead with the firm assurance of your everlasting kindness.

Isaiah 54:6–9

31

Friday

IN THE MORNING

I Delight in Kindness

This is what the LORD says:

"Let not the wise man boast of his wisdom
    or the strong man boast of his strength
    or the rich man boast of his riches,
but let him who boasts boast about this:
    that he understands and knows me,
that I am the LORD, who exercises kindness,
    justice and righteousness on earth,
    for in these I delight,"

                    declares the LORD.

*Lord, help me to brag not about who I am but about who you are.
Never let me run out of words to praise you for your goodness and
your kindness.*

Jeremiah 9:23–24

32

AT NIGHT

I Will Restore Your Fortunes

The LORD will judge his people
    and have compassion on his servants
when he sees their strength is gone
    and no one is left, slave or free.

When you and your children return to the LORD your God and
obey him with all your heart and with all your soul according to
everything I command you today, then the LORD your God will
restore your fortunes and have compassion on you and gather you
again from all the nations where he scattered you. Even if you have
been banished to the most distant land under the heavens, from
there the LORD your God will gather you and bring you back.

*Lord, thank you for assuring us that no one is ever beyond the reach
of your compassion. I pray for those who seem alienated from you.
Give them the grace to turn to you and be healed. Bring them back
from distant lands and restore their fortunes.*

Deuteronomy 32:36; Deuteronomy 30:2–4

Saturday

IN THE MORNING

Clothe Yourself with Compassion

Therefore, as God's chosen people, holy and dearly loved, clothe yourselves with compassion, kindness, humility, gentleness and patience. Bear with each other and forgive whatever grievances you may have against one another. Forgive as the Lord forgave you. And over all these virtues put on love, which binds them all together in perfect unity.

But the fruit of the Spirit is love, joy, peace, patience, kindness, goodness, faithfulness, gentleness and self-control. Against such things there is no law.

Lord, this morning, as I get dressed, help me to envision myself putting on compassion, kindness, humility, gentleness, and patience like a garment. Clothe me in your Spirit so that your goodness is revealed through me.

Colossians 3:12 – 14; Galatians 5:22 – 23

AT NIGHT

I Am the God of All Comfort

Praise be to the God and Father of our Lord Jesus Christ, the Father of compassion and the God of all comfort, who comforts us in all our troubles, so that we can comfort those in any trouble with the comfort we ourselves have received from God. For just as the sufferings of Christ flow over into our lives, so also through Christ our comfort overflows. If we are distressed, it is for your comfort and salvation; if we are comforted, it is for your comfort, which produces in you patient endurance of the same sufferings we suffer. And our hope for you is firm, because we know that just as you share in our sufferings, so also you share in our comfort.

Father of compassion and God of all comfort, please don't let my troubles go to waste. Use them to reshape my heart so that I can comfort others with the comfort you give to me.

2 Corinthians 1:3–7

I WILL REMEMBER THIS

The LORD longs to be gracious to you;
    he rises to show you compassion.
For the LORD is a God of justice.
    Blessed are all who wait for him!

My presence will go with you, and I will give you rest.

The LORD, the LORD, the compassionate and gracious God,
slow to anger, abounding in love and faithfulness.

I will see the goodness of the LORD
    in the land of the living.

Several years ago, Philip Yancey wrote a book entitled *Disappointment with God*. It was an instant bestseller, at least partly because Philip managed to put his finger on a difficulty many have but few admit. In addition to this sense of disappointment with God, I think many of us suffer from a pervasive sense of disappointment with ourselves. Honesty compels us to admit our failure to be the kind of people we want to be.

But is disappointment a bad thing? What if it means we are making progress in the spiritual life because we have finally developed enough trust to admit who we are before God? As I reflected this week, I couldn't help but notice how often

Isaiah 30:18; Exodus 33:14; Exodus 34:6; Psalm 27:13

Scripture links God's compassion with his people's weakness: *In all their distress he too was distressed . . . he remembers that we are dust . . . he will respond to the prayer of the destitute . . . the LORD will surely comfort Zion and will look with compassion on all her ruins . . . the LORD will judge his people and have compassion on his servants when he sees their strength is gone.*

So I will make it my practice to come before the Lord, neither hiding my "ruined places" nor pretending to be strong when I am weak. In the midst of my brokenness, God will show me his compassion.

3

God Speaks Words of Forgiveness

נָשָׂא סָלַח

NASA, SALAH

The Hebrew word *nasa* means to "carry, bear, lift up, or forgive." *Salah* means "to forgive" or "be forgiven." Without forgiveness, our lives would be hopeless because our connection with God would be broken forever. Like buildings wired for electricity, we are "wired" for God. But sin breaks that connection. Without God's forgiveness, we would be like a city that has suddenly gone dark because of an irreparable break in its electrical grid. Because of God's great compassion and his desire to restore our vital connection to him, he graciously extends forgiveness to anyone who asks and who is also willing to extend it to others.

In the New Testament, Paul views forgiveness not just as the removal of guilt for past sins but as deliverance from the power of sin itself. The primary Greek word in the New Testament for divine forgiveness is *aphesis*. It is the life, death, and resurrection of Jesus Christ that brings forgiveness for all who belong to him.

LETTING THE WORD SHAPE ME

This week, as I read through the Scriptures, different thoughts and feelings kept surfacing, arranging themselves into a kind of collage rather than developing neatly into one overarching theme.

A few years ago I heard a friend — a good man — admit that he "felt like the lowest skunk in hell." His self-description seemed laughable though his feelings were not. I think most people — at least the honest ones — will confess that they sometimes do or say things that make them feel rotten and skunk-like. What is it about sin, about human frailty, that makes us feel so ashamed?

I began thinking that sin has a certain trajectory to it. It takes you somewhere, delivering consequences long after you've had the pleasure of committing it. I thought about the consequences of the very first sin — the one the Bible depicts in Eden. I pictured it something like the Big Bang, the theory that says the universe began with an explosion that sent matter careening into space and time. I could imagine that first act of disobedience as a great primordial explosion, expelling everything and everyone from the presence of a holy God. It sent us head over heels into the darkness, unable to find our way back to our life source, fractured, isolated, and divided.

Then I remembered how C. S. Lewis depicts hell in his book *The Great Divorce*. Instead of imagining it as a fiery inferno, he pictures it as a sprawling city into which a drizzly rain constantly falls. The people who populate it are alienated, choosing to live at greater and greater distances from each other. The worst among them move the farthest away, existing in complete isolation and loneliness. My "Big Bang" theory of sin seemed to map rather well with Lewis's depiction of where sin might ultimately lead a person.

But I knew, too, that something else happened after sin blew a hole in the universe. Because God was not content to let things take their natural course, hope entered the picture. In Jesus, I pictured God wrapping his arms around the universe to make it whole again, to reverse the terrible chain reaction that sin had set in motion.

But then, without much warning, my thoughts shifted, taking on a more personal and less cosmic quality. I started thinking about how I had responded during the early months of the Iraq war when Saddam Hussein's two sons were killed. "Yes!" Both times, my response was instinctive, like cheering for my favorite football team. The bad guys had been nailed. I felt like celebrating. But then a discomfiting thought crept in. Was Jesus rejoicing at the death of these two men? I couldn't picture it.

I turned back to the Scriptures. *Do not condemn, and you will not be condemned. Forgive, and you will be forgiven. If you forgive others when they sin against you, your heavenly Father will also forgive you. How many times should you forgive? Seventy-seven times.* These were Jesus' words. But really, I have to forgive rapists and mass murderers?

Then I read the story of a five-year-old from Dorchester, Massachusetts. Two years earlier little Kai Leigh Harriott was sitting on her upstairs porch singing, just singing, when a stray bullet shot through her body and shattered her spine. She would never be able to walk again, not one more step. It seems a man by the name of Anthony Warren was having a bad day, so bad that he fired three shots at Kai's apartment building over an argument he was having with two women inside.

Two years later, sitting in a wheelchair in the Suffolk County courtroom, five-year-old Kai began to cry. Then she looked up at her accuser, "What you done to me was wrong." But her next words surprised everyone, even her mother. Looking around the courtroom, the words came out, soft but sure: "But I still forgive him."

Kai wasn't forgiving a long-distance kind of evil, like the one I had been pondering in Iraq. This was the in-your-face brand, the kind that can ruin your life in the space of a moment. Her act of forgiveness put flesh on the words of Jesus. It showed me what would be required if such a thing ever happened to me or to someone I loved.

This Jesus, he asks so much.

Yes, but he gives so much.

I remembered one of my favorite films, *The Mission*. The scene that haunts me is one that depicts the forgiveness I felt as a new Christian. The story takes place in the eighteenth century, in South America. Robert De Niro plays a brutal slave trader and mercenary by the name of Rodrigo Mendoza. One day, in a flash of rage, he murders his own brother. Unable to deal with the guilt he feels, Rodrigo consults with a Jesuit missionary, who counsels him to devise a penance for himself. Accordingly, the slave trader decides to tether himself to an unbearable burden—a net filled with his own heavy armor, a picture of the life he is trying to leave behind. Then, dragging his armor behind him, he struggles vainly up the side of a cliff—the way to the new mission the Jesuits have established in the jungle. It is a mission to a South American tribe of Indians, many of whom Mendoza had helped enslave.

The scene is painful to watch. Rodrigo, sweating, bloody, and dirty, advances tortuously up the mountainside, frequently stumbling and falling back. I remember holding my breath as I watched him drag the armor up the side of the cliff, aware that the weight of his burden might overpower him at any second, plunging him backward down the mountain. Then suddenly an Indian appears at the cliff's edge. He looks down at Rodrigo. There is a knife in his hand. This is the moment to avenge his people. But instead of avenging himself, he reaches down, cutting the net from Rodrigo's back and then pulling the wretched man up over the edge of the cliff to safety.

It's hard to watch the film and not draw parallels with what it's like to carry around our own unbearable burdens of guilt. I can remember the sense of sheer mercy that came to me years ago when I finally admitted my failings and opened myself to God's forgiveness. As I thought back to how gracious God has been, I felt willing to pray for a change of heart. Instead of cheering the demise of those men in Iraq, I wanted the grace to forgive as I had been forgiven, to let pure justice remain where it belongs — in God's hand.

I thought about the words of Father Lyndon Harris of St. Paul's Chapel, located next to the World Trade Center. Witnessing the attack on September 11 and the grim aftermath, the chaplain kept asking himself the same question: "How in God's name, literally, how in God's name, do we stop this senseless cycle of violence and revenge?" His conclusion: "Forgiveness is the way to say no to the perpetuation of violence for violence. Forgiveness," he says, "is the way to create the future."

It's the way God chose. It's the future I choose — for myself and for my children.

Lord, help me to forgive.

[handwritten notes:]
May 12, 2013 Mother's Day

Aug. #, 2013 Today Dan would be 85 years old (him again) I miss him (Dear Saviour, I will be with dear him again and we shall be with you...)

May 8, 2016 Mother's Day 5-12-13 Alone now for 15 mos. Miss G2+2 so much

Sunday

IN THE MORNING

I Am Slow to Anger

Praise the LORD, O my soul;
  all my inmost being, praise his holy name.
Praise the LORD, O my soul,
  and forget not all his benefits—
who forgives all your sins
  and heals all your diseases,
who redeems your life from the pit
  and crowns you with love and compassion....
The LORD is compassionate and gracious,
  slow to anger, abounding in love....
He does not treat us as our sins deserve
  or repay us according to our iniquities.
For as high as the heavens are above the earth,
  so great is his love for those who fear him;
as far as the east is from the west,
  so far has he removed our transgressions from us.

[handwritten note:] I needed this so much today 5-12-2013 5-8-2016

Lord, help me to remember what you have already done—forgiving all the sins I have ever committed—large or small, hidden or obvious. The power of your forgiveness has healed my past and reshaped my future. Thank you, Lord Jesus.

Psalm 103:1–12

AT NIGHT

I Keep No Record of Your Sins

If you, O LORD, kept a record of sins,
    O Lord, who could stand?
But with you there is forgiveness;
    therefore you are feared.
I wait for the LORD, my soul waits,
    and in his word I put my hope.
My soul waits for the Lord
    more than watchmen wait for the morning,
    more than watchmen wait for the morning.
O Israel, put your hope in the LORD,
    for with the LORD is unfailing love
    and with him is full redemption.
He himself will redeem Israel
    from all their sins.

Lord, thank you for not keeping a record of my sins. Help me to live with the expectation that when you see me, you see someone who belongs to your son. Treat me, O God, not according to my failings but according to your steadfast love.

Psalm 130:3 – 8

Monday

IN THE MORNING

I Will Speak Tenderly

Comfort, comfort my people,
　　says your God.
Speak tenderly to Jerusalem,
　　and proclaim to her
that her hard service has been completed,
　　that her sin has been paid for. ...
A voice of one calling:
"In the desert prepare
　　the way for the LORD;
make straight in the wilderness
　　a highway for our God.
Every valley shall be raised up,
　　every mountain and hill made low;
the rough ground shall become level,
　　the rugged places a plain.
And the glory of the LORD will be revealed,
　　and all mankind together will see it.
　　　　　　　For the mouth of the LORD has spoken."

Lord, my heart is like a wilderness without you, full of rough places and rugged ground. Bring me back to yourself in deeper ways. Let nothing stand in the way of your steady, forgiving love.

Isaiah 40:1–5

AT NIGHT

I Will Not Abandon You

"Our ancestors became arrogant and stiff-necked, and did not obey your commands. They refused to listen and failed to remember the miracles you performed among them. They became stiff-necked and in their rebellion appointed a leader in order to return to their slavery. But you are a forgiving God, gracious and compassionate, slow to anger and abounding in love. Therefore you did not desert them."

For this is what the high and lofty One says—
>   he who lives forever, whose name is holy:
"I live in a high and holy place,
>   but also with him who is contrite and lowly in spirit,
to revive the spirit of the lowly
>   and to revive the heart of the contrite."

Lord, you have never failed or abandoned me even though "stiff-necked" and "stubborn" are words that sometimes apply to me just as they have sometimes applied to your people. Thank you for staying close, for guiding me through the hard times, for sustaining me when I am weak, and for showing me the way when I am confused. Grant me the gift of a lowly, contrite spirit—a heart that will attract your presence and reflect your grace.

Nehemiah 9:16–17 (TNIV); Isaiah 57:15

Tuesday

IN THE MORNING

I Will Not Remember Your Sins

"This is the covenant I will make with the house of Israel
    after that time," declares the LORD.
"I will put my law in their minds
    and write it on their hearts.
I will be their God,
    and they will be my people.
No longer will a man teach his neighbor,
    or a man his brother, saying, 'Know the LORD,'
because they will all know me,
    from the least of them to the greatest,"
                    declares the LORD.
"For I will forgive their wickedness
    and will remember their sins no more."

I run in the path of your commands,
    for you have set my heart free.

Lord, thank you for dealing with the twisted, broken things inside me, not only showing me my sin but enabling me to change. I praise you for not tolerating the distance that existed between us. You dealt with my sin so that I could receive your love.

Jeremiah 31:33–34; Psalm 119:32

AT NIGHT

I Will Heal Your Waywardness

Let us acknowledge the LORD;
  let us press on to acknowledge him.
As surely as the sun rises,
  he will appear;
he will come to us like the winter rains,
  like the spring rains that water the earth.

I will heal their waywardness
  and love them freely,
    for my anger has turned away from them.
I will be like the dew to Israel;
  he will blossom like a lily.
Like a cedar of Lebanon
  he will send down his roots.

Lord, there was a time when I was so very far from you. But you overcame the distance through your strong, forgiving love. How can I doubt your love when the evidence is all around me? Help me to find ways of remembering how good you have been to me by telling others what you have done.

Hosea 6:3; Hosea 14:4–5

Wednesday

IN THE MORNING

I Will Return to You

"Return to me," declares the LORD Almighty, "and I will return to you," says the LORD Almighty.

> Rend your heart
>> and not your garments.
> Return to the LORD your God,
>> for he is gracious and compassionate,
> slow to anger and abounding in love,
>> and he relents from sending calamity.
> Who knows? He may turn and have pity
>> and leave behind a blessing.

Lord, forgive me for blaming you for troubles in my life, as though you and not I are the one who needs to change. Help me to return to you in trust and confidence. Let me experience your overflowing, bountiful love.

Zechariah 1:3; Joel 2:13–14

AT NIGHT

I Will Be Found by You

I have swept away your offenses like a cloud,
> your sins like the morning mist.
Return to me,
> for I have redeemed you.

"You will seek me and find me when you seek me with all your heart. I will be found by you," declares the LORD.

I will build you up and not tear you down; I will plant you and not uproot you. I will give you a heart to know me, that I am the LORD. You will be my people, and I will be your God, for you will return to me with all your heart.

Lord, I love the image of my sins being swept away like an insubstantial mist. Help me to call this image to mind the next time I need to ask your forgiveness. Don't let me give more power to my sin than I do to your forgiveness.

Isaiah 44:22; Jeremiah 29:13 – 14; Jeremiah 24:6 – 7

Thursday

IN THE MORNING

A Bruised Reed I Will Not Break

And you, my child, will be called a prophet of the Most High;
for you will go on before the Lord to prepare the
way for him,
to give his people the knowledge of salvation
through the forgiveness of their sins,
because of the tender mercy of our God,
by which the rising sun will come to us from heaven
to shine on those living in darkness
and in the shadow of death,
to guide our feet into the path of peace.

A bruised reed he will not break,
and a smoldering wick he will not snuff out.

Father, thank you for sending your Son to bring us out of the darkness of our sins and to guide us into the way of peace. Help me today to experience your tender mercy and then to reflect it to those who have been bruised and broken by life.

Luke 1:76–79; Matthew 12:20

AT NIGHT

I Don't Condemn You

"Teacher, this woman was caught in the act of adultery. In the Law Moses commanded us to stone such women. Now what do you say?" They were using this question as a trap, in order to have a basis for accusing him.

But Jesus bent down and started to write on the ground with his finger. When they kept on questioning him, he straightened up and said to them, "If any one of you is without sin, let him be the first to throw a stone at her." . . .

At this, those who heard began to go away one at a time, the older ones first, until only Jesus was left, with the woman still standing there. Jesus straightened up and asked her, "Woman, where are they? Has no one condemned you?"

"No one, sir," she said.

"Then neither do I condemn you," Jesus declared. "Go now and leave your life of sin."

There is now no condemnation for those who are in Christ Jesus.

Jesus, what were you scribbling in the dust as you stooped in front of the woman's accusers? Some say you were writing each man's sins. Thank you for offering rescue rather than condemnation. Help me to stay free as I fight against the sinful habits and patterns that still influence me.

John 8:4–7, 9–11; Romans 8:1

Friday

IN THE MORNING

I Will Heal and Forgive You

I will heal my people and will let them enjoy abundant peace and security. I will bring Judah and Israel back from captivity and will rebuild them as they were before. I will cleanse them from all the sin they have committed against me and will forgive all their sins of rebellion against me. Then this city will bring me renown, joy, praise and honor before all nations on earth that hear of all the good things I do for it; and they will be in awe and will tremble at the abundant prosperity and peace I provide for it.

> Who is a God like you,
>   who pardons sin and forgives transgression?...
> You will again have compassion on us;
>   you will tread our sins underfoot
>   and hurl all our iniquities into the depths of the sea.

"Friend, your sins are forgiven."

Lord, thank you for healing the wounds that sin made in my mind and heart, especially the ones that made me distrustful and fearful. Thank you for changing me and giving me peace. May others know how great you are because of all the good things you have done for me.

Jeremiah 33:6–9; Micah 7:18–19; Luke 5:20

AT NIGHT

I Will Rejoice Over You

Then Jesus told them this parable: "Suppose one of you has a hundred sheep and loses one of them. Does he not leave the ninety-nine in the open country and go after the lost sheep until he finds it? And when he finds it, he joyfully puts it on his shoulders and goes home. Then he calls his friends and neighbors together and says, 'Rejoice with me; I have found my lost sheep.' I tell you that in the same way there will be more rejoicing in heaven over one sinner who repents than over ninety-nine righteous persons who do not need to repent.

"Or suppose a woman has ten silver coins and loses one. Does she not light a lamp, sweep the house and search carefully until she finds it? And when she finds it, she calls her friends and neighbors together and says, 'Rejoice with me; I have found my lost coin.' In the same way, I tell you, there is rejoicing in the presence of the angels of God over one sinner who repents."

Jesus, it's strange to be lost and not know it. But I was. Thank you for pursuing me when I didn't want to have anything to do with you. Never let me wander from you or forget all the ways you have blessed my life.

Luke 15:3–10

Saturday

IN THE MORNING

I Will Forgive You If You Forgive Others

For if you forgive others when they sin against you, your heavenly Father will also forgive you.

Then Peter came to Jesus and asked, "Lord, how many times shall I forgive my brother when he sins against me? Up to seven times?"

Jesus answered, "I tell you, not seven times, but seventy-seven times."

"Forgive, and you will be forgiven. Give, and it will be given to you. A good measure, pressed down, shaken together and running over, will be poured into your lap. For with the measure you use, it will be measured to you."

God, grant me the grace to liberally forgive so that I may be liberally forgiven. Let me celebrate your forgiveness by being generous to those who offend me.

Matthew 6:14 (TNIV); Matthew 18:21–22; Luke 6:37–38

AT NIGHT

I Will Show You How to Pray

"Have faith in God," Jesus answered. "I tell you the truth, if anyone says to this mountain, 'Go, throw yourself into the sea,' and does not doubt in his heart but believes that what he says will happen, it will be done for him. Therefore I tell you, whatever you ask for in prayer, believe that you have received it, and it will be yours. And when you stand praying, if you hold anything against anyone, forgive him, so that your Father in heaven may forgive you your sins."

One day Jesus was praying in a certain place. When he finished, one of his disciples said to him, "Lord, teach us to pray, just as John taught his disciples."

He said to them, "When you pray, say:

" 'Father,
hallowed be your name,
your kingdom come.
Give us each day our daily bread.
Forgive us our sins,
    for we also forgive everyone who sins against us.' "

Lord, you ask hard things: to forgive everyone who sins against us. And yet you have done the harder thing: forgiving child abusers, racists, murderers, adulterers, thieves, gossips, gluttons, and liars — you forgive everyone who repents, including me. Help me to imitate you by extending forgiveness to everyone who hurts me. Give me the grace to leave all final judgment to you.

Mark 11:22 – 25; Luke 11:1 – 4

I WILL REMEMBER THIS

As far as the east is from the west,
   so far has he removed our transgressions from us.

I have swept away your offenses like a cloud,
   your sins like the morning mist.

You will tread our sins underfoot
   and hurl all our iniquities into the depths of the sea.

A bruised reed he will not break,
   and a smoldering wick he will not snuff out.

There will be more rejoicing in heaven over one sinner who repents than over ninety-nine righteous persons who do not need to repent.

I realize that forgiveness can be a process. It begins when I decide to forgive. But it can take time for me to let go of my emotional reactions to what someone has done and my desire to see them suffer for it. But God doesn't have emotional reactions. His forgiveness happens instantly—the moment I repent.

I remember the first time I realized what a positive thing repentance is. The Greek word that often translates "repentance" in the New Testament is *metanoia*. It expresses the idea

Psalm 103:12; Isaiah 44:22; Micah 7:19; Matthew 12:20; Luke 15:7

of turning, of doing an about-face, of heading away from one thing so you can head toward another. It's not just a *turning away* from the disintegrating power of sin but a *turning toward* the creative, life-giving power of God. It's choosing to stand in the light rather than to linger in the darkness.

This week as I read through Scripture I was struck by all the strong, even extreme, images it paints of how God deals with our sins once we repent: he stomps on them; he sweeps them away like a mist; he throws them into the sea; he peels them off and hurls them far from us.

But if this is so, I couldn't help wondering why I sometimes don't feel forgiven even though I've repented. It occurred to me that at least three things might affect my experience. First, I tend to want to punish myself for my failures. Second, my feelings don't always reflect reality. Just because I don't *feel* forgiven doesn't mean God hasn't forgiven me. Third, and this is easy for me to miss, I haven't yet fully repented. Maybe I'm asking God to forgive me not because I am sorry for something I've done or failed to do but simply because I want to protect myself from emotional pain.

I don't like having my weakness exposed. I find it hard to look squarely into my heart, to have my self-illusions punctured. Perhaps by slowing down and allowing myself to feel the pain, not to wallow in it, I will be given the grace to recognize what led to my failure. Maybe God will give me not only his forgiveness but the kind of self-understanding that will help me break out of the habits and patterns that lead to sin.

Perhaps receiving God's forgiveness, like extending it, is for most of us a process rather than an event. Today I pray for the grace to be patient with the process the next time I am tempted to believe that God hasn't really forgiven me.

4

God Speaks Words of Peace

שָׁלוֹם

SHALOM

The Hebrew word for peace is *shalom,* a word with many rich and beguiling implications because it includes the idea not just of the absence of strife and conflict but of wholeness, well-being, health, prosperity, safety, satisfaction, and soundness. When God speaks words of peace, he is speaking words of connection because true peace comes from being in right relationship with him. Peace with God then spreads to other relationships so that we learn to live in harmony with others and in peace with ourselves.

The Greek word for peace is *eirene.* The New Testament reveals Jesus as the source of all peace because his is the sacrifice that has made us whole, restoring our relationship with God and others.

LETTING THE WORD SHAPE ME

I've never been big on New Year's resolutions. To me they're a set up for failure. Like diets. But as January approaches, I've found myself thinking about peace. In fact, I can't stop thinking about it — about my desire for it, about the world's need for it, about what life on earth would be like if we really experienced the peace God promises.

I think, too, about practical steps I might take to make my home a more peaceful place — a place where my children are not constantly bickering and where their mother never yells at them in a misguided effort to get them to stop. Many parents who have adult children assure me that their offspring are now best friends despite prolonged periods of sibling rivalry when they were young. But I don't want to wait another decade for calm to reign in our home.

What can I do to stop the arguing, the competition, the discord? Doesn't Scripture tell us we are to "seek peace and pursue it?" What does that mean on the local level, in my city, on my block, in my home?

One night, after a day filled with endless squabbles, I collapsed on the sofa. All my attempts at peace and reconciliation had failed. I had prayed, encouraged, lectured, punished, and even bribed my children in an effort to teach them to get along. But they still seemed like little alligators, constantly wrestling to see who would come out on top. I felt desperate enough to beg for Supernanny to come to the rescue. So what if our troubles were aired on national television! A little humiliation would be a small price to pay for more peace in our corner of the earth.

Then I thought about Jesus and the land he lived in — Israel. It wasn't a peaceful place either. And today Israel is still not a synonym for peace. Instead, it's a land in which people are being walled off from each other in a desperate effort to keep the peace. The Israelis call the wall a "Separation Barrier," but the Palestinians call it the "Apartheid Wall" or the "Berlin Wall." In fact, when it's finally completed this controversial wall is expected to extend for 403 miles — four times as long as the Berlin Wall!

"Well, if they can do it, I can do it!" I thought. Why not build a wall straight through the house? The children could visit each other on Christmas, on Easter, and on their birthdays. I might even throw in the Fourth of July if they behave. When I confided my brilliant new plan to friends, one laughed and then proceeded to amuse the rest of us with the story of two roommates at a Christian college who had managed to share a tiny dorm room for four years despite their opposite temperaments. They did it by building a wall straight down the middle of their dorm room to define their respective spheres of influence.

Of course, as Robert Frost pointed out in a famous poem nearly a century ago, walls have their drawbacks. "Something there is that doesn't love a wall," he remarked. Of course the "something" Frost is talking about is our need to touch and be touched, to know and be known. We were made for community. Trouble is, we can't seem to touch without hurting each other, can't seem to know without judging each other. And so we put up walls, which only isolate and divide us, creating loneliness and suspicion rather than peace.

So much for my grand solution! As I read God's words, I reflected that peace is not so much a plan as it is a person. I know that real peace, in the Middle East or in Midwest America where

I live, cannot be had without having Christ—inside. I thought about myself. How did I behave when my children were having difficulty?

A passage that has never been a favorite came to mind, the one about having "a gentle and quiet spirit." As I thought about it and prayed about it, I began to wonder if I hadn't misunderstood the instruction all these years. What if this gentle and quiet spirit doesn't describe someone who is timid and passive but someone who has an inner kind of quiet, someone whose peace is so strong that it spreads out to others around her? I wanted to be that kind of person. But the catch was that I needed to let God change me, to calm my anxiety and give me wisdom. Instead of letting my tensions control me, I needed to respond to him with greater trust and deeper obedience.

Here's how one writer describes the biblical ideal of gentleness: "Gentleness means to approach others (including one's enemies) in a humble and caring spirit, not using force to get one's way ... It is included as one of the nine aspects of the fruit of the Spirit in our lives and is part of how wisdom from above goes to work in our lives." I liked that last part especially, about "wisdom from above going to work" in my life. Gentleness, I also realized, is often spoken of in tandem with peace. The peace I longed for could only be produced by the action of God's Spirit in my life.

I remembered the passage from Luke's gospel that portrays Jesus, shortly before his death, weeping over Jerusalem because he could foresee its violent downfall and saying, "If you, even you, had only known on this day what would bring you peace—but now it is hidden from your eyes."

Today I pray that what will bring peace to my home, to my city, and to the troubled regions of our world will not be hidden from my eyes or from yours. Come, Lord Jesus, and reveal yourself as the Peace for which we long. Come and show us the path of peace.

Sunday

IN THE MORNING

I Will Turn My Face toward You

"The LORD bless you
   and keep you;
the LORD make his face shine upon you
   and be gracious to you;
the LORD turn his face toward you
   and give you peace. "

Blessed are those who find wisdom,
   those who gain understanding,
for she is more profitable than silver
   and yields better returns than gold.
She is more precious than rubies;
   nothing you desire can compare with her.
Long life is in her right hand;
   in her left hand are riches and honor.
Her ways are pleasant ways,
   and all her paths are peace.

Lord, wisdom is better than silver and more to be desired than gold. Shine your face on me, and give me the grace to live wisely in this world.

Numbers 6:24–26; Proverbs 3:13–17 (TNIV)

AT NIGHT

I Will Keep You in Perfect Peace

You will keep in perfect peace
    those whose minds are steadfast,
    because they trust in you.

"Though the mountains be shaken
    and the hills be removed,
yet my unfailing love for you will not be shaken
    nor my covenant of peace be removed,"
    says the LORD, who has compassion on you....
All your children will be taught by the LORD,
    and great will be their peace."

Heavenly Father, when everything is shaking around me, hold me steady. Let me remember your unfailing love and your covenant of peace. May my children also learn from you so that they, too, may know your peace.

Isaiah 26:3 (TNIV); Isaiah 54:10, 13 (TNIV)

Monday

IN THE MORNING

I Will Extend Peace like a River

"You will go out in joy
    and be led forth in peace;
the mountains and hills
    will burst into song before you,
and all the trees of the field
    will clap their hands.
Instead of the thornbush will grow the pine tree,
    and instead of briers the myrtle will grow.
This will be for the LORD's renown,
    for an everlasting sign,
    which will not be destroyed."

For this is what the LORD says:

"I will extend peace to her like a river,
    and the wealth of nations like a flooding stream."

*Gracious and loving God, the One who led me out of the darkness
and into the light, thank you for the peace you promise. Let it be like
an ever-flowing river, and I will always proclaim your kindness!*

Isaiah 55:12 – 13; Isaiah 66:12

AT NIGHT

I Will Give Peace to Those Who Trust Me

May the God of hope fill you with all joy and peace as you trust in him.

The fruit of the Spirit is love, joy, peace, patience, kindness, goodness, faithfulness, gentleness and self-control. Against such things there is no law.

The wisdom that comes from heaven is first of all pure; then peace-loving, considerate, submissive, full of mercy and good fruit, impartial and sincere. Peacemakers who sow in peace raise a harvest of righteousness.

Lord, peace comes from you. Help me to stop looking for it in other places. Give me the grace to make room in my soul for your Spirit. Fill me with the wisdom that is pure and peace-loving, merciful and considerate. Make me a peacemaker like you.

Romans 15:13; Galatians 5:22–23; James 3:17–18

Tuesday

IN THE MORNING

My Peace Will Guard Your Heart

Rejoice in the Lord always. I will say it again: Rejoice! Let your gentleness be evident to all. The Lord is near. Do not be anxious about anything, but in everything, by prayer and petition, with thanksgiving, present your requests to God. And the peace of God, which transcends all understanding, will guard your hearts and your minds in Christ Jesus.

When the LORD takes pleasure in anyone's way,
    he causes their enemies to make peace with them.

Lord, grant me a rejoicing spirit. May I be a person who is gentle and not harsh, calm and not anxious. Take pleasure in me and bring me peace, I pray.

Philippians 4:4–7; Proverbs 16:7 (TNIV)

AT NIGHT

I Am the Lord of Peace

Now may the Lord of peace himself give you peace at all times and in every way.

If you follow my decrees and are careful to obey my commands, I will send you rain in its season, and the ground will yield its crops and the trees of the field their fruit. Your threshing will continue until grape harvest and the grape harvest will continue until planting, and you will eat all the food you want and live in safety in your land.

I will grant peace in the land, and you will lie down and no one will make you afraid.

Lord, may your peace characterize my life in every way. No matter who threatens, no matter what happens, be near to me, and I will know your peace.

2 Thessalonians 3:16; Leviticus 26:3–6

11 year bonnWERsey y 9-11-2001

Wednesday

IN THE MORNING

I Will Train You

Grace and peace be yours in abundance.

Endure hardship as discipline; God is treating you as his children. For what children are not disciplined by their father? If you are not disciplined — and everyone undergoes discipline — then you are not legitimate children at all. Moreover, we have all had parents who disciplined us and we respected them for it. How much more should we submit to the Father of spirits and live! Our parents disciplined us for a little while as they thought best; but God disciplines us for our good, that we may share in his holiness. No discipline seems pleasant at the time, but painful. Later on, however, it produces a harvest of righteousness and peace for those who have been trained by it.

Lord, "discipline" is not my favorite word. It doesn't sound very tender. But when you discipline it is always for my good. Thank you for treating me, not as a stranger, but as a child in your family. I trust the way you are working in my life.

1 Peter 1:2; Hebrews 12:7–11 (TNIV)

72 Today was Diane and my 64th wedding anniversary. I miss him so very much, I will see him again in heaven. 'Twas Diane he went to Jesus

AT NIGHT

I Will Make Peace Your Governor

My people will live in peaceful dwelling places,
>	in secure homes,
>	in undisturbed places of rest.

I will make peace your governor
>	and righteousness your ruler.
No longer will violence be heard in your land,
>	nor ruin or destruction within your borders,
but you will call your walls Salvation
>	and your gates Praise.

You have filled my heart with greater joy
>	than when their grain and new wine abound.
I will lie down and sleep in peace,
>	for you alone, O LORD,
>	make me dwell in safety.

Lord, you want to govern my life with peace. Help me to entrust the future to you — whether my future is on earth or in heaven. You give me the grace to lie down and sleep in peace, confident that wherever I am I will dwell in safety.

Isaiah 32:18; Isaiah 60:17 – 18; Psalm 4:7 – 8

Thursday

IN THE MORNING

I Have Made Peace for You

Therefore, since we have been justified through faith, we have peace with God through our Lord Jesus Christ.

But he was pierced for our transgressions,
    he was crushed for our iniquities;
the punishment that brought us peace was upon him,
    and by his wounds we are healed.

The fruit of righteousness will be peace;
    the effect of righteousness will be quietness and confidence forever.

Jesus, I thank you for the peace in my soul that came the moment I gave my life to you. You were crushed so that I wouldn't be. I praise you, Lord.

Romans 5:1; Isaiah 53:5; Isaiah 32:17

AT NIGHT

I Am the Prince of Peace

The LORD is Peace.

For to us a child is born,
    to us a son is given,
    and the government will be on his shoulders.
And he will be called
    Wonderful Counselor, Mighty God,
    Everlasting Father, Prince of Peace.

God, you are healing, wholeness, prosperity, satisfaction, perfection, protection, harmony, and well-being. You are everything I need. Lord, you are peace.

Judges 6:24; Isaiah 9:6

Friday

IN THE MORNING

I Will Guide You in the Way of Peace

How beautiful on the mountains
    are the feet of those who bring good news,
who proclaim peace,
    who bring good tidings,
    who proclaim salvation,
who say to Zion,
    "Your God reigns!"

I will make a covenant of peace with them; it will be an everlasting covenant. I will establish them and increase their numbers, and I will put my sanctuary among them forever. My dwelling place will be with them; I will be their God, and they will be my people.

Lord, thank you for being the "good news" we can celebrate, for making a way when there was no way—out of our darkness and into the peace of your presence. You are a God of unfailing love, and we are grateful to be your people.

Isaiah 52:7; Ezekiel 37:26–27

AT NIGHT

I Myself Am Peace

And there were shepherds living out in the fields nearby, keeping watch over their flocks at night. An angel of the Lord appeared to them, and the glory of the Lord shone around them, and they were terrified. But the angel said to them, "Do not be afraid. I bring you good news of great joy that will be for all the people. Today in the town of David a Savior has been born to you; he is the Messiah, the Lord. This will be a sign to you: You will find a baby wrapped in cloths and lying in a manger."

Suddenly a great company of the heavenly host appeared with the angel, praising God and saying,

"Glory to God in the highest heaven,
    and on earth peace to those on whom his favor rests."

Lord, you are the peace for which all men and women long. Open our eyes to your presence. Help us to perceive your glory.

Luke 2:8–14 (TNIV)

Saturday

IN THE MORNING

My Peace I Give You

While they were still talking about this, Jesus himself stood among them and said to them, "Peace be with you."

They were startled and frightened, thinking they saw a ghost. He said to them, "Why are you troubled, and why do doubts rise in your minds? Look at my hands and my feet. It is I myself! Touch me and see."

Peace I leave with you; my peace I give you. I do not give to you as the world gives. Do not let your hearts be troubled and do not be afraid.

Lord, calm my anxious, troubled heart. When I am afraid, remind me to turn my attention away from the things I fear so that I can look at you.

Luke 24:36–39; John 14:27

AT NIGHT

Let My Peace Rule in Your Hearts

The mind controlled by the Spirit is life and peace.

Finally, brothers and sisters, whatever is true, whatever is noble, whatever is right, whatever is pure, whatever is lovely, whatever is admirable — if anything is excellent or praiseworthy — think about such things. Whatever you have learned or received or heard from me, or seen in me — put it into practice. And the God of peace will be with you.

Let the peace of Christ rule in your hearts, since as members of one body you were called to peace.

Lord, forgive me for allowing worldly desires to dominate. Shape my mind and heart through your all-powerful Spirit. Teach me to think your thoughts after you, and let your peace rule inside me regardless of what is happening around me.

Romans 8:6; Philippians 4:8–9 (TNIV); Colossians 3:15

I WILL REMEMBER THIS

"Though the mountains be shaken
    and the hills be removed,
yet my unfailing love for you will not be shaken
    nor my covenant of peace be removed,"
    says the LORD, who has compassion on you.

The fruit of the Spirit is love, joy, peace, patience, kindness, goodness, faithfulness, gentleness and self-control. Against such things there is no law.

I will lie down and sleep in peace,
    for you alone, O LORD,
    make me dwell in safety.

The LORD is Peace.

I know one thing about peace — it's the way the world was meant to be, the way God intended it to operate. Peace was to be the normal state of things just like health was to be the normal condition of our bodies.

Consider for a moment a simple, if rough, comparison. Imagine a world in which every single car that has ever been made breaks down constantly. There are lots of different models. Some are sleek and beautiful. Others are simple and inexpensive. But

Isaiah 54:10; Galatians 5:22–23; Psalm 4:8; Judges 6:24

all of them have one thing in common. None of them can travel more than a hundred miles without breaking down. Wouldn't the people in that world seem justified in concluding that it is simply a car's nature to break down all the time? However justified their conclusions might seem, they would be dead wrong.

Something similar happens in our world when we draw the conclusion that strife is normative. Divorce, domestic violence, turf wars, church splits, border skirmishes, terrorism, war. It's easy to throw up our hands and think we can't do a thing about it. But, if that is so, why does the Bible exhort us to "seek peace and pursue it"? Why are we told to pray for peace? And why does Jesus call the peacemakers blessed? Don't we need to do more in this world than give up? Don't we have to imitate the costly example of Christ who with his sacrifice brought us back to God—the One who is the source of all peace?

I pray today that God will make me a peacemaker, a person who wants what Christ wants and is not afraid to make the necessary sacrifices. May God forgive my apathy and my fear and help me to reflect his heart in this world.

5

God Speaks Words of Strength

גְּבוּרָה עֹז

GEBURAH, OZ

The Hebrew Scriptures make it clear that God is the source of all strength. His power is so great that no power in heaven or on earth can compete with it. Moreover, his love impels him to use his power on behalf of his people, to save those who hope in him.

The Hebrew word *geburah* is commonly translated as "power," "strength," or "might." *Oz* is another Hebrew word, often translated "strength," "strong," "power," "might," or "mighty." Anyone who grew up watching reruns of *The Wizard of Oz* on television may be interested to know that *oz* is often used to describe God's strength.

The Greek word *kratos* is translated "power, might, strength" in the New Testament. Ultimately, Jesus is presented as the strongest of all men, the One who through his death and resurrection has overpowered Satan, ultimately freeing us from the devastating consequences of sin.

Remember that God's Word is powerful, living and active, able to accomplish far more than we can even ask or imagine. This week let it transform your understanding of how God wants to reveal his strength in you and for you.

LETTING THE WORD SHAPE ME

We were lying in bed talking.

"I'm stronger than any of the boys in our school," I modestly announced.

"You are," my sister agreed.

"I bet I could arm wrestle a high school guy and win," I said.

"You could," she affirmed.

"I'm probably way stronger even than a college kid!" I said in a crescendo of self-confidence. Remarkably, my eight-year-old sister said yes, I probably was.

My illusions of grandeur had been sparked that day on the school playground, where I had challenged a sixth-grade boy to a contest to see who could chin themselves the most times on the monkey bars. His twelve-year-old body, wiry though it was, was no match against a skinny first-grader who also happened to be a megalomaniac. I watched him leave the field in disgrace, shoulders sagging, humiliated by a six-year-old girl!

That memory captures the sum total of my early understanding of strength. I thought it was entirely a contest of bodies.

It wasn't long before I would learn the truth—that life can knock the stuffing out of you, not once but repeatedly. My early cockiness soon faded, replaced by a sense that the world wasn't as safe or pleasant as I had thought. As it sooner or later does to all of us, it began to dawn on me that the strength that really mattered was internal rather than external.

So I tried to be strong—inside. But that only meant bottling things up, putting a wall around my feelings, appearing strong regardless of how I felt. To some degree hiding works.

You can fool people. Sometimes you can even fool yourself. But feelings have a way of asserting themselves, of creating pressure cracks in even the best-constructed walls. No matter how hard I looked for strength inside myself, I could never find the degree of strength I needed. That came later, with my conversion. With my admitting my weakness and my need before God. It came as Christ poured out his gracious love, unbending and untwisting what had been broken and bent inside me by sin — my sin and the sins of others. That process continues.

So I came to these words about God's strength with a desire to experience more of his help on a daily basis. And as I read the words, I began asking myself what strength is for. What did God expect me to do with the strength he promises to give? Does he strengthen me so that I can feel better about myself or so that I can look better to others? I doubted it. Surely that kind of interpretation was a throwback to the egocentric views of my childhood.

I thought about Jesus. His strength was expressed overtly through the miracles he performed. But it was also expressed in surprising ways, in ways that made him look weak. Who but a weak man, a man who had been overpowered by others, would allow himself to be violently whipped and executed? He certainly looked weak to his friends, all of whom fled the moment he was arrested. It wasn't until later that they understood how strong Jesus was, that his strength was not to be measured against the strength of wicked people but against the power of wickedness itself.

So that's what strength is for. To enable us to resist the distorting, misshaping power of sin, to make us more like Jesus so that inch by inch and life by life the gospel will be preached and the world will be transformed.

In so many ways, the strength that Christ has portrayed and that God promises is counter-intuitive, a contradiction to the world's idea of strength. It is the power to control our appetites rather than to let them control us. It is the ability to endure rather than to run away. It is the quick instinct to take refuge in God rather than to trust in our own abilities or resources. It is the humility to ask God daily for what we need rather than to work ourselves into a frenzy trying to construct the perfect safety net. It is the ability to keep gazing at God even when trouble and fear assails us. It is the patience to wait rather than to run on ahead. It is the faith to keep praying no matter what. It is the decision to put others first and ourselves last. It is the grace to believe that nothing is impossible because we belong to God. It is the strength to be more than we are because God is more than we imagine. It is the power to run and not grow weary, to walk and not be faint, to ground ourselves in God's might and his power to help and to save.

Every week I attend a small group, composed of friends whose purpose it is to encourage each other to become more like Jesus. I love this group. Each member is like a sister to me. But I have to confess that I feel like a fraud whenever it's my turn to read one of the promises we make for the week ahead: *By God's grace, I will strive mightily against sin and will do deeds of love and mercy.* The words sound awkward, so noble and knight-like, so romantic and grandiose — so unlike the person I am. So I deal with my discomfort by stressing to myself the part about God's grace. I know that without it I will fail. But now it strikes me that I am going to have to embrace the part about *striving mightily* too because otherwise what is God's grace for?

So as I brood over God's words, I pray for the grace to know just how strong he is and how generous. Rather than hoarding his strength, he shares it gladly, for as Scripture says, "The eyes of the LORD range throughout the earth to strengthen those whose hearts are fully committed to him." I pray, today, that his glance will rest on me.

Sunday

IN THE MORNING

I Will Be Your Strength

O LORD be gracious to us;
>we long for you.
Be our strength every morning,
>our salvation in time of distress.

My soul is weary with sorrow;
>strengthen me according to your word.

In you, O LORD, I have taken refuge;
>let me never be put to shame;
>deliver me in your righteousness.
Turn your ear to me,
>come quickly to my rescue;
be my rock of refuge,
>a strong fortress to save me.

*Every day I have need of your strength, Lord. Help me to know you
as refuge and fortress, a rock upon which I can stand no matter how
difficult life becomes.*

Isaiah 33:2; Psalm 119:28; Psalm 31:1–2

AT NIGHT

I Will Support You

O my Strength, I watch for you;
   you, O God, are my fortress, my loving God.

Whom have I in heaven but you?
   And earth has nothing I desire besides you.
My flesh and my heart may fail,
   but God is the strength of my heart
   and my portion forever.

He reached down from on high and took hold of me;
   he drew me out of deep waters.
He rescued me from my powerful enemy,
   from my foes, who were too strong for me.
They confronted me in the day of my disaster,
   but the LORD was my support.
He brought me out into a spacious place;
   he rescued me because he delighted in me.

One thing God has spoken,
   two things have I heard:
that you, O God, are strong,
   and that you, O Lord, are loving.

Lord, I praise you not only for your strength but also for your love.
Please blend strength and love in me, so that I can show others who
you are.

Psalm 59:9–10; Psalm 73:25–26; 2 Samuel 22:17–20; Psalm 62:11–12

Monday

IN THE MORNING

I Want to Give You Courage and Confidence

"Be strong and courageous. Do not be afraid or discouraged because of the king of Assyria and the vast army with him, for there is a greater power with us than with him. With him is only the arm of flesh, but with us is the LORD our God to help us and to fight our battles."

> The LORD is my light and my salvation —
> whom shall I fear?
> The LORD is the stronghold of my life —
> of whom shall I be afraid?
> When the wicked advance against me
> to devour me,
> it is my enemies and my foes
> who will stumble and fall.
> Though an army besiege me,
> my heart will not fear;
> though war break out against me,
> even then will I be confident.

Lord, steady my heart, so that when life is difficult, I will not give in to the temptation to think you have rejected me. May I remember that strength comes from living in your presence and relying on your faithfulness.

2 Chronicles 32:7–8; Psalm 27:1–3 (TNIV)

AT NIGHT

I Will Keep You Strong to the End

Strengthen the feeble hands,
    steady the knees that give way;
say to those with fearful hearts,
    "Be strong, do not fear;
your God will come,
    he will come with vengeance;
with divine retribution
    he will come to save you.

The bolts of your gates will be iron and bronze,
    and your strength will equal your days.

Christ will keep you strong to the end, so that you will be blameless on the day of our Lord Jesus Christ. God, who has called you into fellowship with his Son Jesus Christ our Lord, is faithful.

Lord, you know how quickly I can swing from being assured of your presence to being certain of your absence. I'm so tired of being pushed around by circumstances. Help me to stop wavering between feelings of faith and anxiety. Give me the peace that comes from believing you are willing and able to keep me strong to the end.

Isaiah 35:3–4; Deuteronomy 33:25; 1 Corinthians 1:8–9

Tuesday

IN THE MORNING

I Will Never Leave You

Do not be afraid or terrified because of them, for the LORD your God goes with you; he will never leave you nor forsake you.

March on, my soul; be strong!

I am still confident of this:
>   I will see the goodness of the LORD
>   in the land of the living.
Wait for the LORD;
>   be strong and take heart
>   and wait for the LORD.

"Be strong, all you people of the land," declares the LORD, "and work. For I am with you," declares the LORD Almighty. "This is what I covenanted with you when you came out of Egypt. And my Spirit remains among you. Do not fear."

Lord, you promise that you will never leave nor forsake me. I promise the same to you. When things go wrong—and they will go wrong—help me to feel neither helpless nor hopeless, but confident that you are who you say you are.

Deuteronomy 31:6; Judges 5:21b; Psalm 27:13–14; Haggai 2:4–5

AT NIGHT

I Will Sustain You

For the eyes of the Lord range throughout the earth to strengthen those whose hearts are fully committed to him.

My hand will sustain him;
   surely my arm will strengthen him.

So do not fear, for I am with you;
   do not be dismayed, for I am your God.
I will strengthen you and help you;
   I will uphold you with my righteous right hand.
All who rage against you
   will surely be ashamed and disgraced;
those who oppose you
   will be as nothing and perish.
Though you search for your enemies,
   you will not find them.
Those who wage war against you
   will be as nothing at all.

Father, I know you watch over those who belong to you. Defend me, Lord, when enemies advance. Do not let me give in to fear. Instead, strengthen my heart and I will give you praise.

2 Chronicles 16:9; Psalm 89:21; Isaiah 41:10–12

Wednesday

IN THE MORNING

I Will Guide You Always

And if you spend yourselves in behalf of the hungry
and satisfy the needs of the oppressed,
then your light will rise in the darkness,
and your night will become like the noonday.
The LORD will guide you always;
he will satisfy your needs in a sun-scorched land
and will strengthen your frame.
You will be like a well-watered garden,
like a spring whose waters never fail.

This is what the Sovereign LORD, the Holy One of Israel, says:

"In repentance and rest is your salvation,
in quietness and trust is your strength."

Lord, help me to spend myself not on myself but on others, especially the needy of this world. Give me an eye to understand how they see things and wisdom to know how to help.

Isaiah 58:10–11; Isaiah 30:15

AT NIGHT

I Will Fill You with My Strength

"The people of Jerusalem are strong, because the LORD Almighty is their God."

The name of the LORD is a strong tower;
the righteous run to it and are safe.

For the foolishness of God is wiser than human wisdom, and the weakness of God is stronger than human strength.

Then Peter said, "Silver or gold I do not have, but what I have I give you. In the name of Jesus Christ of Nazareth, walk." Taking the lame man by the right hand, he helped him up, and instantly the man's feet and ankles became strong. He jumped to his feet and began to walk ... All the people were astonished and came running to them in the place called Solomon's Colonnade. When Peter saw this, he said to them: "Men of Israel, why does this surprise you?... By faith in the name of Jesus, this man whom you see and know was made strong. It is Jesus' name and the faith that comes through him that has given this complete healing to him, as you can all see."

Lord, I don't have enough money to solve all the problems I see around me. But I do have your Spirit living in me. Help me not to limit the ways you want to work through me so that others might begin to know who you are.

Zechariah 12:5; Proverbs 18:10; 1 Corinthians 1:25 (TNIV); Acts 3:6–8, 11–12, 16

Thursday

IN THE MORNING

There's Nothing You Can't Do When I Strengthen You

I can do everything through him who gives me strength.

Then Moses and the Israelites sang this song to the LORD:

"I will sing to the LORD,
    for he is highly exalted.
The horse and its rider
    he has hurled into the sea.
The LORD is my strength and my song;
    he has become my salvation.
He is my God, and I will praise him,
    my father's God, and I will exalt him."

Hear, O Israel: The LORD our God, the LORD is one. Love the LORD your God with all your heart and with all your soul and with all your strength.

Lord, I want to believe with St. Paul that I can do all things as long as I am drawing on your strength. Forgive me for my cowardice and my unwillingness to take risks. Give me a bigger vision of what you want to do through me.

Philippians 4:13; Exodus 15:1–2; Deuteronomy 6:4–5

AT NIGHT

Your Way Is Not Hidden from Me

Why do you say, O Jacob,
    and complain, O Israel,
"My way is hidden from the LORD;
    my cause is disregarded by my God"?
Do you not know?
    Have you not heard?
The LORD is the everlasting God,
    the Creator of the ends of the earth.
He will not grow tired or weary,
    and his understanding no one can fathom.
He gives strength to the weary
    and increases the power of the weak.
Even youths grow tired and weary,
    and young men stumble and fall;
but those who hope in the LORD
    will renew their strength.
They will soar on wings like eagles;
    they will run and not grow weary,
    they will walk and not be faint.

Lord, how easy it is to underestimate your love, to think that you are tired of hearing about my problems. Forgive me for acting as though you don't know or don't care. Help me to stop complaining and start believing that you give strength to the weary and that you increase the power of the weak. I am weak, Lord, renew my strength.

Isaiah 40:27–31

Friday

IN THE MORNING

I Will Shield You

For God did not give us a spirit of timidity, but a spirit of power, of love and of self-discipline.

The LORD is my strength and my shield;
    my heart trusts in him, and I am helped.
My heart leaps for joy
    and I will give thanks to him in song.
The LORD is the strength of his people,
    a fortress of salvation for his anointed one.

Thank you, God, for giving me the strength I need every day — the strength to love, to believe, to resist evil, to stand firm, to show kindness, to do what is right even when I am afraid or upset. I trust that you will always be my strength.

2 Timothy 1:7; Psalm 28:7–8

AT NIGHT

I Am a Rock You Can Lean On

As for God, his way is perfect;
    the word of the LORD is flawless.
He is a shield
    for all who take refuge in him.
For who is God besides the LORD?
    And who is the Rock except our God?
It is God who arms me with strength
    and makes my way perfect.
He makes my feet like the feet of a deer;
    he enables me to stand on the heights.
He trains my hands for battle;
    my arms can bend a bow of bronze.
You give me your shield of victory;
    you stoop down to make me great.

Lord, thank you for friends and family who are a support to me. But none of them is a rock like you are. You are the only one who is completely dependable, in whom there is no weakness and no instability. I thank you for being the Rock in whom I can take refuge and find strength.

2 Samuel 22:31–36

Saturday

IN THE MORNING

I Am Your Fortress, Your Loving God

But I will sing of your strength,
in the morning I will sing of your love;
for you are my fortress,
my refuge in times of trouble.
O my Strength, I sing praise to you;
you, O God, are my fortress, my loving God.

The LORD gives strength to his people;
the LORD blesses his people with peace.

Blessed are those whose strength is in you,
who have set their hearts on pilgrimage.
As they pass through the Valley of Baca,
they make it a place of springs;
the autumn rains also cover it with pools.
They go from strength to strength,
till each appears before God in Zion.

Father, let me rise each day, asking with confidence for the strength I need. Make me strong against worry, financial pressure, selfishness, and fear. Strengthen me to do your will so that I will not only have peace but spread it to others.

Psalm 59:16–17; Psalm 29:11; Psalm 84:5–7

AT NIGHT

I Want You to Seek My Face

Look to the LORD and his strength;
    seek his face always.

Surely God is my salvation;
    I will trust and not be afraid.
The LORD, the LORD, is my strength and my song;
    he has become my salvation.
With joy you will draw water
    from the wells of salvation.

. . . the joy of the LORD is your strength.

Lord, sometimes I look for strength in the wrong places — placing my hope in others, trying to control circumstances and people, thinking that money will keep me safe. But surely you are my strength and my song. Help me to seek your face always and there to find strength.

Psalm 105:4; Isaiah 12:2–3; Nehemiah 8:10

I WILL REMEMBER THIS

Whom have I in heaven but you?
    And earth has nothing I desire besides you.
My flesh and my heart may fail,
    but God is the strength of my heart
    and my portion forever.

One thing God has spoken,
    two things have I heard:
that you, O God, are strong,
    and that you, O Lord, are loving.

This is what the Sovereign LORD, the Holy One of Israel, says:

"In repentance and rest is your salvation,
    in quietness and trust is your strength."

The name of the LORD is a strong tower;
    the righteous run to it and are safe.

The LORD is my strength and my song;
    he has become my salvation.
He is my God, and I will praise him,
    my father's God, and I will exalt him.

Psalm 73:25–26; Psalm 62:11–12; Isaiah 30:15; Proverbs 18:10; Exodus 15:2

I remember how startled I was by a friend's offhanded comment one day. "God doesn't like guys' legs," she declared.

"What?" I couldn't believe God would even weigh in on the topic.

"Listen," she continued, quoting from Psalm 147, "God's 'pleasure is not in the strength of the horse, nor his delight in the legs of a man.'"

She smiled, enjoying her little joke.

Of course the passage makes perfect sense when you read the conclusion: "The LORD delights in those who fear him, who put their hope in his unfailing love." The point, of course, is that human strength isn't impressive. From God's perspective, the strongest person who ever lived is just a featherweight.

I think Scripture is clear. No matter how smart or determined or gifted I may be, I don't have the stamina, confidence, hope, wit, wisdom, purity, peace, perspective, patience, money, or health to handle all the challenges I will face. The only way to obtain the kind of strength I need is to trust in God's unfailing love, drawing conclusions for my life that are based on trust and not on fear.

I want to adopt St. Paul's pugnacious faith. Confident that God's grace would be sufficient for every challenge — hunger, thirst, sleeplessness, bandits, violence, shipwreck, slander, persecution, and more — Paul affirmed: "I will boast all the more gladly about my weaknesses, so that Christ's power may rest on me. That is why, for Christ's sake, I delight in weaknesses, in insults, in hardships, in persecutions, in difficulties. For when I am weak, then I am strong" (2 Corinthians 12:9–10). Paul could have looked at all the obstacles he faced as evidence that

God wasn't with him and didn't love him. But, instead, he did the reverse, believing that God's presence would become more obvious in the midst of hardship.

My list of troubles seems feeble compared to Paul's, but here's a few of the challenges I currently face: worry for my children, patience with their persistent struggles, concern for other family members, fatigue, slight depression that comes from living in a place where the sun doesn't shine much, pressing deadlines, chronic back pain, and a lack of time, money and wisdom. My list is trivial in light of Paul's and in light of so many others, but it can still seem overwhelming at times, tempting me to view it as evidence that God doesn't care.

Today I pray for the grace to boast of my weakness as I learn a deeper kind of trust. I pray in the months ahead that God will do the impossible, that he will enable me to delight in my hardships and to rejoice in the trade he is inviting me to make—my weakness for his strength.

6

God Speaks Words of Protection

צֵל שָׁמַר נָצַר

TSEL, SHAMAR, NATSAR

One of the Hebrew words used in the Old Testament to convey the notion of protection is *sel*, which can be translated "shadow." As the psalmist in Psalm 91 says, "Whoever dwells in the shelter of the Most High will rest in the shadow of the Almighty." *Tsel* is often used to refer to a kind of protective shadow. The implication is that if we dwell close to the Lord, believing and obeying him, we will be overshadowed by his presence, hidden so that no evil will destroy us.

The Hebrew word *shamar* can be translated "to keep," "to guard," or "to watch over," as in the words of Psalm 121: "He who watches over Israel will neither slumber nor sleep." Another Hebrew verb, *natsar*, is often translated as "keep," "guard," "protect," or "preserve," as in Psalm 31: "The LORD preserves the faithful, but the proud he pays back in full." Jesus invoked this same psalm just before he died on the cross, commending himself into God's protective care by saying, "Father, into your hands, I commit my spirit" (Luke 23:46).

When you listen to God's words of protection, keep in mind that he stands watch over those who love him and keep to his ways.

LETTING THE WORD SHAPE ME

This week I woke up to an ice storm raging outside. School was canceled, so I celebrated the unexpected gift of a leisurely morning with another cup of coffee as I watched the morning news. There would be no rush to roust my children from their beds, no mad dash to school. After the news I began flipping through channels to see what else was on. I stopped at a program I had never seen before, arrested by the words of a familiar psalm, one I had just been reading and thinking about. I checked the impulse to keep channel surfing and instead listened as a pastor told a remarkable story. He began by reading these verses from Psalm 91 aloud:

> Whoever dwells in the shelter of the Most High
>   will rest in the shadow of the Almighty.
> They say of the LORD, "He is my refuge and my fortress,
>   my God, in whom I trust."
> Surely he will save you
>   from the fowler's snare
>   and from the deadly pestilence.
> He will cover you with his feathers,
>   and under his wings you will find refuge;
>   his faithfulness will be your shield and rampart.
> You will not fear the terror of night,
>   nor the arrow that flies by day,
> nor the pestilence that stalks in the darkness,
>   nor the plague that destroys at midday.
> A thousand may fall at your side,
>   ten thousand at your right hand,
>   but it will not come near you. (TNIV)

The pastor went on to say that he had felt God directing his attention to the psalm one morning though he had no idea why. Later that day, on the way to his favorite restaurant, he had the distinct impression that God was also telling him to skip lunch. So instead of going into the restaurant, he merely parked his car outside and spent a little time praying. To concentrate better, he leaned back in his seat and then closed his eyes.

But his concentration shifted when he heard someone tapping on the window. A stranger was peering through the glass asking for help. Reaching into his pocket for the money he had meant to spend on lunch, the pastor rolled down the window, handed it to the man, and began speaking to him about the love of Christ. As the two men talked, the stranger seemed to open up. The man admitted he was tired of living like a gangbanger and said he was ready to change. When the two men parted, the pastor handed the stranger his card and then invited him to church.

That night when the pastor switched on the evening news, he was startled by a photo that flashed across the screen. The newscaster warned viewers that the man was an escaped convict who had killed three people. He was considered extremely dangerous. It was, of course, the man who had tapped on the pastor's window just hours before. Immediately, the words of the psalmist flooded his mind: *He will cover you with his feathers, and under his wings you will find refuge.*

I was impressed not only by the story of God's protection but by the fruit of that pastor's obedience. Who knew what evil was averted because of the pastor's kindness? Because of his obedience, he was in the right place at the right time with the right resources to sow seeds of the gospel into a dangerous life, a life that may one day change because of the love of Christ.

But what about people God hasn't protected? Innocent people? Faithful people? People who seem to be doing the Lord's work?

A month ago I received an urgent email from a friend who works for the Association for a More Just Society (AJS), a Christian organization dedicated to helping the poorest and most vulnerable members of Honduran society. His email asked for prayers on behalf of a Honduran lawyer by the name of Dionisio Diaz Garcia, who had received an anonymous death threat. Dionisio's specialty was representing poor people whose rights had been violated by employers. Many of them had been forced to work overtime without pay, others had been subjected to illegal salary deductions, and yet others had been framed for crimes they didn't commit. Dionisio had been repeatedly threatened by one particular company that had been charged with several labor violations.

As soon as I read my friend's email, I sent up a quick prayer: *God please protect Dionisio. Surround him with your care and protection.*

Then I promptly forgot about it.

Six days later, my friend emailed me with the news: *Earlier this morning AJS labor lawyer Dionisio Diaz Garcia was shot to death by masked gunmen near the Supreme Court of Honduras.*

Dionisio had been on his way to argue a case in court when two men on a motorcycle pulled up next to his pickup truck and shot him to death. A good man, fighting for a good cause had been suddenly and brutally slaughtered, leaving his wife and six-year-old son without a husband and father.

Three days later, another death threat. This time directed at the president of AJS's board of directors, who received a text message on his cell phone that read: *you are the next.*

Since then, Christians from around the world have mobilized to pray for the protection of all those who are working for AJS. As I join my prayers to theirs, I remember God's promises in Scripture. But I also remember that the outcome of any given struggle cannot be predicted even though the attitude of God toward those who love him can be. He stands guard over us just as the psalmist in Psalm 121:7–8 declares:

The LORD will keep you from all harm—
> he will watch over your life;
the LORD will watch over your coming and going
> both now and forever more.

Though wickedness may flourish for a time, it is ultimately true, as Scripture assures us, that "when calamity comes, the wicked are brought down, but even in death the righteous have a refuge" (Proverbs 14:32).

As I ponder God's words of protection, I ask for a deeper kind of confidence in God's ability to watch over me and those I care about. May I without anxiety leave the decision of whether he will protect my body or only my soul in his loving, all-powerful hands. And may my confidence in his watchful care free me from fear so I can be flexible and faithful whatever God asks.

Sunday

IN THE MORNING

I Hear Your Prayers

I sought the LORD, and he answered me;
  he delivered me from all my fears.
Those who look to him are radiant;
  their faces are never covered with shame.
This poor man called, and the LORD heard him;
  he saved him out of all his troubles.
The angel of the LORD encamps around those who fear
  him,
  and he delivers them.
Taste and see that the LORD is good;
  blessed are those who take refuge in him.
Fear the LORD, you his holy people,
  for those who fear him lack nothing.
The lions may grow weak and hungry,
  but those who seek the LORD lack no good thing.

*Lord, thank you for hearing my prayers and delivering me from my
fears. Help me to live with a sense of awe in your presence, seeking
always to hear and to do your Word. May your angels encircle me,
keeping me safe.*

Psalm 34:4–10 (TNIV)

AT NIGHT

No Harm Will Overtake You

Whoever dwells in the shelter of the Most High
    will rest in the shadow of the Almighty.
They say of the LORD, "He is my refuge and my fortress,
    my God, in whom I trust."...
He will cover you with his feathers,
    and under his wings you will find refuge ...
A thousand may fall at your side,
    ten thousand at your right hand,
    but it will not come near you ...
For he will command his angels concerning you
    to guard you in all your ways;
they will lift you up in their hands,
    so that you will not strike your foot against a stone ...
"Because they love me," says the LORD, "I will rescue
    them."

Lord, teach me what it means to dwell in your shelter and to take refuge under your wings. Let me see your shadow — evidence that you are near, watching over me.

Psalm 91:1 – 2, 4, 7, 11 – 12, 14 (TNIV)

Monday

IN THE MORNING

I Am Your Hiding Place

You forgave
  the guilt of my sin.
Therefore let all the faithful pray to you
  while you may be found;
surely the rising of the mighty waters
  will not reach them.
You are my hiding place;
  you will protect me from trouble
  and surround me with songs of deliverance.
I will instruct you and teach you in the way you should go;
  I will counsel you with my loving eye on you.

Lord, you are my hiding place and strong deliverer. Help me to take shelter in you today by seeking and following your counsel. Thank you for your promised protection and your faithful care.

Psalm 32:5–8 (TNIV)

AT NIGHT

I Neither Slumber Nor Sleep

I lift up my eyes to the hills—
  where does my help come from?
My help comes from the LORD,
  the Maker of heaven and earth.
He will not let your foot slip—
  he who watches over you will not slumber;
indeed, he who watches over Israel
  will neither slumber nor sleep.
The LORD watches over you—
  the LORD is your shade at your right hand;
the sun will not harm you by day,
  nor the moon by night.
The LORD will keep you from all harm—
  he will watch over your life;
the LORD will watch over your coming and going
  both now and forevermore.

Lord, you are a perfect Father. Your attention never strays from those you love. Help me to lie down in peace, knowing that you are guarding me.

Psalm 121

Tuesday

IN THE MORNING

I Am at Your Right Hand

Keep me safe, O God,
 for in you I take refuge ...
I will praise the LORD, who counsels me;
 even at night my heart instructs me.
I have set the LORD always before me.
 Because he is at my right hand,
 I will not be shaken.
Therefore my heart is glad and my tongue rejoices;
 my body also will rest secure,
because you will not abandon me to the grave,
 nor will you let your Holy One see decay.
You have made known to me the path of life;
 you will fill me with joy in your presence,
 with eternal pleasures at your right hand.

*Lord, when trouble comes, help me to look up at you and not down
at all the things that are making life difficult. Instruct my heart and
guide my steps, remind me that you are at my right hand, and I will
praise you.*

Psalm 16:1, 7–11

114

AT NIGHT

I Am the Shepherd Who Keeps You Safe

The LORD is my shepherd, I shall not be in want.
    He makes me lie down in green pastures,
he leads me beside quiet waters,
    he restores my soul.
He guides me in paths of righteousness
    for his name's sake.
Even though I walk
    through the valley of the shadow of death,
I will fear no evil,
    for you are with me;
your rod and your staff,
    they comfort me.
You prepare a table before me
    in the presence of my enemies.
You anoint my head with oil;
    my cup overflows.
Surely goodness and love will follow me
    all the days of my life,
and I will dwell in the house of the LORD
    forever.

Lord, your strength and your power — your rod and your staff — they comfort me. Even the memory of your faithfulness helps keep me calm. When I am afraid, help me to picture you as you are — a fiercely loving Shepherd, ready to ward off whatever threatens me.

Psalm 23

Wednesday

IN THE MORNING

I Have Stored Up Good Things for You

How great is your goodness,
    which you have stored up for those who fear you,
which you bestow in the sight of all
    on those who take refuge in you.
In the shelter of your presence you hide them
    from all human intrigues;
you keep them safe in your dwelling
    from accusing tongues.
Praise be to the LORD,
    for he showed me the wonders of his love
    when I was in a city under siege.

Lord, forgive me for underestimating your goodness. When life is difficult, I have sometimes blamed you—as though you intend to harm rather than to help me. Sanctify my mind and my imagination so that instead of misjudging you, I can perceive you as you are—strong and wise, loving and protective. Reveal to me the wonders of your love.

Psalm 31:19–21 (TNIV)

AT NIGHT

My Wisdom Will Watch Over You

Do not forsake wisdom, and she will protect you;
    love her, and she will watch over you.

When calamity comes, the wicked are brought down,
    but even in death the righteous have a refuge.

Those whose walk is blameless are kept safe,
    but those whose ways are perverse will fall into the pit.

Those who trust in themselves are fools,
    but those who walk in wisdom are kept safe.

Follow my decrees and be careful to obey my laws, and you will live safely in the land. Then the land will yield its fruit, and you will eat your fill and live there in safety.

Lord, you have already shown me the way to live. Forgive the times when I have preferred my will over yours. Help me to obey you in matters small and large, and be my refuge when calamity comes.

Proverbs 4:6; Proverbs 14:32; Proverbs 28:18 (TNIV); Proverbs 28:26 (TNIV); Leviticus 25:18–19

Thursday

IN THE MORNING

Trust in Me at All Times

The righteous may have many troubles,
>   but the LORD delivers them from them all;
he protects all their bones,
>   not one of them will be broken.
Evil will slay the wicked;
>   the foes of the righteous will be condemned.
The LORD redeems his servants;
>   no one who takes refuge in him will be condemned.

"Holy Father, protect them [Jesus' disciples] by the power of your name—the name you gave me—so that they may be one as we are one. While I was with them, I protected them and kept them safe by that name you gave me ... My prayer is not that you take them out of the world but that you protect them from the evil one."

Lord, I remember what happened to you on the cross. They pierced your side but did not break any of your bones. You had many troubles but you showed us the way to overcome them all. I trust that you will protect me and deliver me now and forever, amen.

Psalm 34:19–22 (TNIV); John 17:11–12, 15

AT NIGHT

I Will Reach Down and Help You

The LORD is my rock, my fortress and my deliverer;
    my God is my rock, in whom I take refuge.
    He is my shield and the horn of my salvation,
        my stronghold.
I call to the LORD, who is worthy of praise,
    and I am saved from my enemies.
The cords of death entangled me;
    the torrents of destruction overwhelmed me.
The cords of the grave coiled around me;
    the snares of death confronted me.
In my distress I called to the LORD;
    I cried to my God for help.
From his temple he heard my voice;
    my cry came before him, into his ears ...
He reached down from on high and took hold of me;
    he drew me out of deep waters.
He rescued me from my powerful enemy,
    from my foes, who were too strong for me.
They confronted me in the day of my disaster,
    but the LORD was my support.
He brought me out into a spacious place;
    he rescued me because he delighted in me.

Lord, even in my worst disaster, you are there, strong and loving. I know that you will hear my call. When I cry out to you with all my heart, you will answer me.

Psalm 18:2–6, 16–19

Friday

IN THE MORNING

I Am Your Shield of Victory

You, O LORD, keep my lamp burning;
 my God turns my darkness into light.
With your help I can advance against a troop;
 with my God I can scale a wall.
As for God, his way is perfect;
 the word of the LORD is flawless.
He is a shield
 for all who take refuge in him.
For who is God besides the LORD?
 And who is the Rock except our God?
It is God who arms me with strength
 and makes my way perfect.
He makes my feet like the feet of a deer;
 he enables me to stand on the heights.
He trains my hands for battle;
 my arms can bend a bow of bronze.
You give me your shield of victory,
 and your right hand sustains me;
 you stoop down to make me great.

Lord, you build me up and make me strong. With your help I can do anything you ask me to. Give me a courageous heart to fight the battles that come to those who belong to you.

Psalm 18:28–35

AT NIGHT

I Will Send My Love and Faithfulness

Have mercy on me, O God, have mercy on me,
     for in you my soul takes refuge.
I will take refuge in the shadow of your wings
     until the disaster has passed.
I cry out to God Most High,
     to God, who fulfills his purpose for me.
He sends from heaven and saves me,
     rebuking those who hotly pursue me;
     God sends his love and his faithfulness.

The eternal God is your refuge,
     and underneath are the everlasting arms.

*Lord, I ask you to fulfill your purpose for my life. Don't let anything
or anyone obstruct your plan. When trouble comes, hide me in the
shelter of your wings.*

Psalm 57:1 – 3; Deuteronomy 33:27

Saturday

IN THE MORNING

I Will Give You Wisdom

For the LORD gives wisdom,
    and from his mouth come knowledge and understanding.
He holds victory in store for the upright,
    he is a shield to those whose walk is blameless,
for he guards the course of the just
    and protects the way of his faithful ones.
Then you will understand what is right and just
    and fair — every good path.
For wisdom will enter your heart,
    and knowledge will be pleasant to your soul.
Discretion will protect you,
    and understanding will guard you.

Lord, help me to understand what is right and just and fair — to follow every good path. May discretion protect me and understanding watch over me. Keep me safe as I seek to follow you.

Proverbs 2:6–11

122

AT NIGHT

I Will Wipe Away Your Tears

You have been a refuge for the poor,
    a refuge for the needy in their distress,
a shelter from the storm
    and a shade from the heat.
For the breath of the ruthless
    is like a storm driving against a wall
    and like the heat of the desert.
You silence the uproar of foreigners;
    as heat is reduced by the shadow of a cloud,
    so the song of the ruthless is stilled.
On this mountain the Lord Almighty will prepare
    a feast of rich food for all peoples,
a banquet of aged wine —
    the best of meats and the finest of wines.
On this mountain he will destroy
    the shroud that enfolds all peoples,
the sheet that covers all nations;
    he will swallow up death forever.
The Sovereign Lord will wipe away the tears
    from all faces.

Lord, you offer the deepest kind of protection. No matter what happens in this life I know that you will one day wipe away the last of my tears. You will still the song of my ruthless enemy, destroying death forever. I praise you, my faithful God.

Isaiah 25:4–8 (TNIV)

I WILL REMEMBER THIS

Whoever dwells in the shelter of the Most High
    will rest in the shadow of the Almighty.
They say of the Lᴏʀᴅ, "He is my refuge and my fortress,
    my God, in whom I trust."

He will not let your foot slip—
    he who watches over you will not slumber;
indeed, he who watches over Israel
    will neither slumber nor sleep.

The eternal God is your refuge,
    and underneath are the everlasting arms.

Do not forsake wisdom, and she will protect you;
    love her, and she will watch over you.

As I thought about God's promise to watch over and guard those
who belong to him, I recalled several instances in my own life in
which God has made good on this promise.

1. When I was ten, I nearly drove a boat full speed into a
   dock because I had become distracted by something. I
   looked up just in time to swerve and miss the dock.

Psalm 91:1–2 (TNIV); Psalm 121:3–4; Deuteronomy 33:27; Proverbs 4:6

2. On my twelfth birthday I was almost run over by a car when crossing a busy street near my home.

3. When I was fourteen, the car I was riding in was broadsided by a truck that had run a red light. It would have killed me had I been sitting in the left rear seat rather than the right rear seat.

4. When I was in my early thirties, a speeding car missed a friend and me by an inch as we jogged across a busy parkway. (We both nearly suffered heart attacks, however!)

5. When I was in my late thirties on a business trip to London, I stepped off the curb and was nearly run over by a car. (I had forgotten they drive on the opposite side of the street.)

6. When I was forty-nine, I nearly plunged off a stairwell into empty space when my attic was being converted to office space. I was so busy admiring the remodeling job that I had forgotten that the stair railing had been temporarily removed.

Ok, you might suspect that I suffer from Attention Deficit Disorder, or a chronic case of carelessness, and you might be right. But I thank God for faithfully protecting me from myself lo these many years. In fact, it occurs to me that much of the time I need protection not so from outside threats but from ones that come from within. It also occurs to me that the most precious part of any human being is the part that is capable of living forever. More even than my body, my soul is what primarily needs God's watchful protecting care. I need protection from anything that would threaten my faith and my faithfulness.

Jesus must have foreseen the harm that many of his followers would suffer for love of him. But listen to how he prayed for his disciples just shortly before his death: "I will remain in the world no longer, but they are still in the world, and I am coming to you. Holy Father, protect them by the power of your name ... My prayer is not that you take them out of the world but that you protect them from the evil one" (John 17:11, 15). He was praying, not so much from evils that would threaten their bodies but from ones that might harm their souls.

Knowing this, I still ask God to keep me and those I love from physical harm. But whether he answers in precisely the way I want him to, I know it is true, as the psalmist proclaims, that my help comes from the Lord, who watches over me. He will not let my foot slip. Nor will he slumber or sleep.

7

God Speaks Words of Love and Mercy

HESED

Hesed, which occurs about 250 times in the Hebrew Scriptures, is a word rich in promise, one that is best understood within the context of the covenant relationship God has with his people. It can be translated as "love," "kindness," "unfailing love," "loving-kindness," "faithfulness," "devotion," or "mercy." You could say that *hesed* is what tethers us to God, for without mercy the relationship between a holy God and sinful people could not be maintained. *Hesed* is the word used in God's self-description in Exodus 34:6–7: "The LORD, the LORD, the compassionate and gracious God, slow to anger, abounding in *love* and faithfulness." God's *hesed* is most fully expressed in the life and death of Jesus Christ, who through his mercy saves us.

Eleos is the Greek word that corresponds most closely to the Hebrew word *hesed*. Jesus of Nazareth is God's mercy made visible. He shows God's faithfulness by saving us from our sins so that we may have eternal life in unbroken fellowship with God. "Have mercy on us!" is a plea repeated by blind men, a tax collector, and desperate parents, all crying out to Jesus for his help.

LETTING THE WORD SHAPE ME

The other day one of my children banged through the front door, a frown on her face, her arms crossed defensively.

"What's wrong?" I asked.

"Caroline can't play! She's going out to dinner with her parents. They don't want me to play with her—ever!" The words came out like an audible pout. "Why are they always going out? They should check with me before they go anywhere! They must not want me to play with her!"

I tried to calm my daughter by reminding her that families need time together and that she shouldn't take her friend's absence personally. But the torrent continued. She was steamed—a mini-tornado full of frustrated, whirling energy swirling in on itself.

It struck me that many of us go through life like mini-whirlwinds, with our energy tightly focused inward, as though we are the universe's true center. I remembered an extreme example of this. It happened a few years ago when a friend was speaking to a high school class about abortion. Janet had carefully explained what abortion was, pointing out that it involved ending a human life. Then she discussed adoption and presented specific suggestions for how a problem pregnancy could be dealt with without resorting to abortion. During the question and answer period that followed, a girl raised her hand and said: "I still don't get it. What's the difference?"

After having discussed abortion and adoption in some detail, Janet was puzzled by the remark. What was so hard about understanding the difference? Probing further, she discovered what the girl was really asking: "What difference does it make *to me* if I abort my baby or give it up for adoption. In either case, *I* still don't have the baby."

Talk about a failure of empathy! The only person whose feelings this girl could imagine was herself.

Some of us are like tiny swirling tornadoes, too absorbed in our own thoughts, needs, and desires to take notice of anyone else. This image captures for me a picture of how distorted and destructive our lives can become when God is not at the center with his healing, stabilizing grace. But before I could close the lid on such thoughts, something happened. A letter in the mail. An urgent phone call. News of a friend in a public position who had been guilty of a serious moral indescretion. Suddenly my own thoughts began swirling. What would happen next? I imagined the fallout, all the negative consequences. And then I let myself wonder if there might be an upside. More specifically, might circumstances work out in a way that might benefit me? I could think of none, so I quickly pushed the thought aside and began praying for my friend. How difficult life must be for her.

It wasn't until the day after that I felt a surge of sympathy as I thought of what the next few days might hold. The ugliness of the situation hit me full face.

I wasn't repulsed by what my friend had supposedly done wrong but by how I had first responded to news of her difficulty. It seems I am just one more swirling, self-absorbed tornado, quite capable of spinning her own destructive thoughts.

This, in fact, was my state of mind—the sense of my need for God raw and real—when I began to read his words of mercy.

"It is not the healthy who need a doctor, but the sick. But go and learn what this means: 'I desire mercy, not sacrifice.' For I have not come to call the righteous, but sinners." (Matthew 9:12–13)

But when the kindness and love of God our Savior appeared, he saved us, not because of righteous things we had done, but because of his mercy. (Titus 3:4–5)

Seek the LORD while he may be found;
call on him while he is near.
Let the wicked forsake their ways
and the unrighteous their thoughts.
Let them turn to the LORD, and he will have mercy on
them,
and to our God, for he will feely pardon.

"For my thoughts are not your thoughts,
neither are your ways my ways,"
declares the LORD. (Isaiah 55:6–8, TNIV)

Then I read a brief essay that painted a similar picture but employed a different image. The writer talked about a kind of crust that forms over the human heart. It happens when we direct our life toward what he called "partial attractions" — things like money, sex, security, position, or power. Jesus, he said, came to rip away the "crust" of our hearts so that we could know him as our true desire.

No wonder the Lord comes across in the gospel as someone who is not always very nice. Instead of smoothing things over, Jesus often seems to deliberately stir things up. Take the cases of the Samaritan woman and Pontius Pilate. The writer pointed out that Jesus "is abrasive and even hurtful, because he is not delicate with the crust; he does not connive with it or humor it. This crust is a barrier between him and the heart, and he will never respect or politely tolerate any such barrier. The Samaritan woman's barrier was doubt that true love and friendship could exist. Pilate's barrier was power and position."

I wondered about my own heart and about the heart of my friend. How encrusted had each become by the "partial attractions" we have pursued? I prayed for myself and for her, asking God to come with his mercy and tear away the barriers in our hearts that keep us from enshrining him there.

Sunday

IN THE MORNING

I Will Not Be Angry Forever

"Return, faithless Israel," declares the LORD,
   "I will frown on you no longer,
for I am merciful," declares the LORD,
   "I will not be angry forever."

If from there you seek the LORD your God, you will find him if you look for him with all your heart and with all your soul. When you are in distress and all these things have happened to you, then in later days you will return to the LORD your God and obey him. For the LORD your God is a merciful God; he will not abandon or destroy you or forget the covenant with your forefathers, which he confirmed to them by oath.

Lord, you have promised never to forget, abandon, or destroy me. Help me to base my life on truth — the truth of who you are and how you look at me — with eyes of mercy and not of condemnation.

Jeremiah 3:12; Deuteronomy 4:29–31

AT NIGHT

My Love Will Satisfy You

The Lord is full of compassion and mercy.

O God, you are my God,
    earnestly I seek you;
my soul thirsts for you,
    my body longs for you,
in a dry and weary land
    where there is no water.
I have seen you in the sanctuary
    and beheld your power and your glory.
Because your love is better than life,
    my lips will glorify you.
I will praise you as long as I live,
    and in your name I will lift up my hands.
My soul will be satisfied as with the richest of foods;
    with singing lips my mouth will praise you.

Lord, you have shown your love to me in countless ways. Help me to base my life, not on my weakness but on the strength of your love. Teach me to rely on the love you have for me because it is better than life.

James 5:11; Psalm 63:1–5

Monday

IN THE MORNING

I Am Rich in Mercy

To those who have been called, who are loved by God the Father and kept by Jesus Christ:

Mercy, peace and love be yours in abundance.

Because of his great love for us, God, who is rich in mercy, made us alive with Christ even when we were dead in transgressions—it is by grace you have been saved. And God raised us up with Christ and seated us with him in the heavenly realms in Christ Jesus, in order that in the coming ages he might show the incomparable riches of his grace, expressed in his kindness to us in Christ Jesus. For it is by grace you have been saved, through faith—and this not from yourselves, it is the gift of God.

Lord, everything good in my life has come as a gift from your hand. And the best gift is this—that you gave your Son to save me. Thank you for the mercy that defines my life and keeps me connected to you now and forever.

Jude 1:1–2; Ephesians 2:4–8

AT NIGHT

You Can Trust in My Unfailing Love

Turn, O LORD, and deliver me;
    save me because of your unfailing love.

My enemy will say, "I have overcome him,"
    and my foes will rejoice when I fall.
But I trust in your unfailing love;
    my heart rejoices in your salvation.
I will sing to the LORD,
    for he has been good to me.

Keep yourselves in God's love as you wait for the mercy of our
Lord Jesus Christ.

*Lord, sin weakens me and makes me vulnerable to all kinds of evil.
Today I cry out for mercy. Extend your hand and raise me up.
Let me triumph over my foes through your faithful help. Keep me
grounded in your love.*

Psalm 6:4; Psalm 13:4–6; Jude 1:21

Tuesday

IN THE MORNING

I Fill the Hungry with Good Things

And Mary said:

"My soul glorifies the Lord
    and my spirit rejoices in God my Savior,
for he has been mindful
    of the humble state of his servant.
From now on all generations will call me blessed,
    for the Mighty One has done great things for me—
    holy is his name.
His mercy extends to those who fear him,
    from generation to generation.
He has performed mighty deeds with his arm;
    he has scattered those who are proud in their
               inmost thoughts.
He has brought down rulers from their thrones
    but has lifted up the humble.
He has filled the hungry with good things
    but has sent the rich away empty.

*Lord, you never forget those who belong to you. Instead you pour
out your mercy, filling us with good things. Fill me today with a
sense of your presence and with gratitude for the gift of your Son.*

Luke 1:46–53

AT NIGHT

What Do You Want Me to Do For You?

As Jesus approached Jericho, a blind man was sitting by the roadside begging. When he heard the crowd going by, he asked what was happening. They told him, "Jesus of Nazareth is passing by."

He called out, "Jesus, Son of David, have mercy on me!"

Those who led the way rebuked him and told him to be quiet, but he shouted all the more, "Son of David, have mercy on me!"

Jesus stopped and ordered the man to be brought to him. When he came near, Jesus asked him, "What do you want me to do for you?"

"Lord, I want to see," he replied.

Jesus said to him, "Receive your sight; your faith has healed you." Immediately he received his sight.

Jesus, I will not stop crying out to you no matter what anyone else may think or say. I know my need and where my help comes from—from you, my Lord and Savior.

Luke 18:35–43

Wednesday

IN THE MORNING

I Listen to the Needy

To some who were confident of their own righteousness and looked down on everybody else, Jesus told this parable: "Two men went up to the temple to pray, one a Pharisee and the other a tax collector. The Pharisee stood up and prayed about himself: 'God, I thank you that I am not like other men—robbers, evildoers, adulterers—or even like this tax collector. I fast twice a week and give a tenth of all I get.'

"But the tax collector stood at a distance. He would not even look up to heaven, but beat his breast and said, 'God, have mercy on me, a sinner.'

"I tell you that this man, rather than the other, went home justified before God. For everyone who exalts himself will be humbled, and he who humbles himself will be exalted."

Lord, only the empty can be filled, only the hungry can be fed. I am sinful and weak, in need of your mercy. Feed me and fill me with your loving-kindness, I pray.

Luke 18:9–14

AT NIGHT

I Will Freely Pardon You

Seek the LORD while he may be found;
    call on him while he is near.
Let the wicked forsake their ways
    and the unrighteous their thoughts.
Let him turn to the LORD, and he will have mercy on him,
    and to our God, for he will freely pardon.
"For my thoughts are not your thoughts,
    neither are your ways my ways,"
                    declares the LORD.
"As the heavens are higher than the earth,
    so are my ways higher than your ways
    and my thoughts than your thoughts."

For I desire mercy, not sacrifice,
    and acknowledgment of God rather than burnt offerings.

Lord, why I am always surprised by your kindness and amazed by your goodness? Help me to stop thinking of you as a giant-sized human being and to start perceiving who you really are. I praise you for valuing mercy more than sacrifice and for freely forgiving all who turn to you — including me.

Isaiah 55:6–9; Hosea 6:6

Thursday

IN THE MORNING

I Desire Mercy

While Jesus was having dinner at Matthew's house, many tax collectors and "sinners" came and ate with him and his disciples. When the Pharisees saw this, they asked his disciples, "Why does your teacher eat with tax collectors and 'sinners'?"

On hearing this, Jesus said, "It is not the healthy who need a doctor, but the sick. But go and learn what this means: 'I desire mercy, not sacrifice.' For I have not come to call the righteous, but sinners."

Mercy triumphs over judgment!

Lord, help me not to look down on people whose lives are a mess. Instead, make me an instrument of your mercy, remembering that I, like them, am among those in need of your healing grace.

Matthew 9:10–13; James 2:13

AT NIGHT

I Sympathize with Your Weakness

One of the criminals who hung there hurled insults at him: "Aren't you the Christ? Save yourself and us!"

But the other criminal rebuked him. "Don't you fear God," he said, "since you are under the same sentence? We are punished justly, for we are getting what our deeds deserve. But this man has done nothing wrong."

Then he said, "Jesus, remember me when you come into your kingdom."

Jesus answered him, "I tell you the truth, today you will be with me in paradise."

Therefore, since we have a great high priest who has gone through the heavens, Jesus the Son of God, let us hold firmly to the faith we profess. For we do not have a high priest who is unable to sympathize with our weaknesses ... Let us then approach the throne of grace with confidence, so that we may receive mercy and find grace to help us in our time of need.

Lord, one of your last acts before your death was to show mercy. Indeed your whole life was an act of mercy — sharing our sorrows and bearing our grief. Thank you for sympathizing with our weakness and enabling us to approach you with confidence so that we might find help in our time of need.

Luke 23:39–43; Hebrew 4:14–16

Christmas Day
2015

Friday

IN THE MORNING

Be Merciful as I Am Merciful

He has shown all you people what is good.
And what does the LORD require of you?
To act justly and to love mercy
and to walk humbly with your God.

If you love those who love you, what credit is that to you? Even sinners love those who love them. And if you do good to those who are good to you, what credit is that to you? Even sinners do that. And if you lend to those from whom you expect repayment, what credit is that to you? Even sinners lend to sinners, expecting to be repaid in full. But love your enemies, do good to them, and lend to them without expecting to get anything back. Then your reward will be great, and you will be children of the Most High, because he is kind to the ungrateful and wicked. Be merciful, just as your Father is merciful.

Thank you for all the mercy you have already shown me. Help me to remember that the kind of mercy you extend is "pass along mercy." Let me remember that the next time someone hurts or offends me. Give me eyes of mercy and a heart of mercy to do your will.

Micah 6:8 (TNIV); Luke 6:32–36 (TNIV)

AT NIGHT

I Have Loved You with an Everlasting Love

I have loved you with an everlasting love;
    I have drawn you with loving-kindness.

Who is a God like you,
    who pardons sin and forgives the transgression
    of the remnant of his inheritance?
You do not stay angry forever
    but delight to show mercy.

Blessed are the merciful,
    for they will be shown mercy.

Lord, the next time I am tempted to respond with anger and judgment, remind me of your promise to bless the merciful. Instead of harshness, let me respond with your love. Give me the grace to change.

Jeremiah 31:3; Micah 7:18; Matthew 5:7

Saturday

IN THE MORNING

I Am Powerful Yet Kind

Who among the gods is like you, O Lord?
  Who is like you—
      majestic in holiness,
      awesome in glory,
      working wonders?
You stretched out your right hand
  and the earth swallowed them.
In your unfailing love you will lead
  the people you have redeemed.

David said ... "Let me fall into the hands of the Lord, for his mercy is very great; but do not let me fall into human hands."

Lord, you are so much better than we could ever ask or imagine—a God who is majestic not only for his power but also for his mercy. No matter what I have done, let me trust myself to you.

Exodus 15:11–13; 1 Chronicles 21:13 (TNIV)

AT NIGHT

I Am for You

For surely it is not angels he [Jesus] helps, but Abraham's descendants. For this reason he had to be made like his brothers in every way, in order that he might become a merciful and faithful high priest in service to God, and that he might make atonement for the sins of the people. Because he himself suffered when he was tempted, he is able to help those who are being tempted.

You are a chosen people, a royal priesthood, a holy nation, a people belonging to God, that you may declare the praises of him who called you out of darkness into his wonderful light. Once you were not a people, but now you are the people of God; once you had not received mercy, but now you have received mercy.

Lord, thank you for making us who we cannot be in our own power—a chosen people, a royal priesthood, a holy nation. Help us to join ourselves to others who every day depend on your sustaining grace. May we together praise you for calling us out of darkness and bringing us into your light.

Hebrews 2:16–18; 1 Peter 2:9–10

I WILL REMEMBER THIS

I will sing to the LORD,
>for he has been good to me.

Keep yourselves in God's love as you wait for the mercy of our Lord Jesus Christ.

He has shown all you people what is good.
>And what does the LORD require of you?
To act justly and to love mercy
>and to walk humbly with your God.

"Jesus, Son of David, have mercy on me!"

I like the story of the blind beggar sitting on the roadside begging when Jesus came walking by. You remember him, don't you? He's the guy everybody tried to hush up. I'm guessing that all that hollering made people feel uneasy.

Maybe some in the crowd had seen the man begging before. Perhaps they had dropped a coin or two into his cup. But they had probably never faced the rawness of his need, never imagined what it would be like to live inside his skin. Maybe they thought the blind man was asking too much of Jesus. Why couldn't he simply accept his lot in life? Why make a fuss in front of everyone?

Psalm 13:6; Jude 1:21; Micah 6:8 (TNIV); Luke 18:38

But Jesus didn't seem offended by the man's behavior. Instead of scolding him, Jesus stopped and asked what he wanted.

I think the story is about more than one thing. It's about crying out to God in our need, our misery, our mess, and not caring how we look or sound to others. It's about praying persistently, asking repeatedly for the help we need. And it's also about a new kind of seeing — the kind that only comes through faith.

The blind man professed his faith in Jesus by using a messianic title, shouting out: "Jesus, *Son of David*, have mercy on me!" Though blind, he had the spiritual vision to perceive who Jesus was. He knew what Jesus could do for him. And so Jesus did it — restoring the man's physical sight and then commending him for his spiritual insight — his faith.

Today I pray that the God who is rich in mercy will make me rich in faith. I want to live in a way that celebrates his mercy — extending it to others as I receive it from him.

8

God Speaks Words of Blessing and Provision

בָּרַךְ רָאָה

BARAK, RA-AH

The Hebrew word *barak* means "to bless," while *baruk* means "blessed," and *beraka* means "blessing." In the Bible, the act of blessing involves pronouncing something good and then bringing it about. By implication a blessing is only as effective as the one who has uttered it. In the case of God, a blessing is an empowering word that always accomplishes its purpose. A blessing can also be a prayer that invokes good or that seeks to avert or overcome evil. In the Hebrew Scriptures, blessings were passed from generation to generation, as when Isaac blessed his son Jacob and when Jacob, at the end of his life, blessed his own sons.

The Hebrew word *ra-ah* is often translated "to see." In a few cases it is translated "provide." The most significant instance of this occurs in Genesis 22, when Abraham is about to sacrifice Isaac. At the last minute God provides a ram to be sacrificed instead. Unlike human beings, whose lives unfold in time, God exists outside of time. To him the future is as clearly seen as the present and the past. By seeing the future with perfect clarity, he can anticipate our needs and thus provide for us. Similarly, the English word "provision" is composed of two Latin words that mean "to see beforehand."

LETTING THE WORD SHAPE ME

This year the first day of spring was marked by a sudden and prolonged thunderstorm. I watched the light show from behind the steering wheel of my car as rain lashed the windshield and lightning streaked across the sky followed by great rolling booms of thunder. One of my children was certain our car was about to blow up. I tried to comfort her, assuring her that we were safe and that she would soon be home, snuggling in her own warm bed.

The storm came just as I had been spending time praying about God's words of provision. Truthfully, my prayers were messy and undignified. Lately, I had been worried about finances. I had recently made a large investment, perhaps too large. Now I wondered if I had been overly eager to profit from an opportunity I should have passed up. I felt especially guilty because I had made the decision quickly, without spending much time in prayer. In fact, I had ignored the unease I had felt whenever I had prayed. How could I expect God's help now? I imagined him shaking his head, arms folded tightly across his chest, and frowning down from on high as I suffered the consequences.

It occurred to me that my attitude toward God was something like my daughter's attitude toward the thunderstorm. We were both cringing, as though at any moment we might be taken out by a sudden bolt from above.

I realize that storms are not always a bad thing. The Bible portrays thunder and lightning in both positive and negative terms, as signs of both divine provision and divine judgment. So how should I look at my situation? Was the cloud half full or was it half empty?

The next day I drove past a church with a sign outside that read: "God Delights in You!" It encouraged me — for a moment.

But I couldn't help wondering, does God delight in everyone who drives by this church? What if Ted Bundy or Saddam Hussein were to drive by? Or what if the Klu Klux Klan were to stage a march past it?

I couldn't dislodge the sense that God was displeased. Then something happened at work—or didn't happen. I couldn't find an important permissions file. I had painstakingly obtained permission to use people's stories in an upcoming book, but now I couldn't find the file and it would be difficult and time-consuming to reconstruct it. I searched my office three times but it wasn't anywhere. So I prayed and asked friends to pray. I kept searching but still couldn't locate it.

Then something worse happened. My children's nanny quit. As any working mother will tell you, losing someone who helps care for your children is traumatic. But Kathy is so much more than a nanny. She's the prototype of the Proverbs 31 woman. She takes care of the house, watches my children when I have to work or travel, and does a million and one things to keep our lives running smoothly. She also prays for us. She's more like a sister than an employee. What would we do without her?

Through all this I kept up a running dialogue with God. "Lord, forgive me for spending beyond my means ... If I've run ahead of you, Lord, I repent ... Please provide for our finances ... Lord, you know I need that file. Please help me find it ... Lord, help Kathy find the position she needs, with more hours than I can give her ... God, give me wisdom for the year ahead.... What arrangements should I make for the girls?" And on and on. Sometimes I felt peaceful as I prayed, sure that God was going to help me. At other times I felt anxious, as though I were addressing a skinflint rather than a loving Father.

Then I came across a story by Sharon Jeffus, a widow who talked about how disappointed she was when a particular relationship didn't work out as she had hoped. One morning she found herself sitting in church. As she waited for the service to begin, her head was filled with thoughts that she later described as silly and childish:

> "God you hate me ... you don't care." ... Then a young man came and sat right in front of me and right on the back of his T-Shirt were the words, "So you think I don't love you." And a picture of Christ on the cross.

Like Sharon, I, too, am sometimes guilty of entertaining silly and childish thoughts about God. Perhaps I had made some mistakes. Maybe my priorities weren't in perfect order. God may have been displeased with certain choices I had made, but he had neither abandoned nor condemned me, just as I would never abandon or condemn one of my own children because of something they had done. No, he had invested too much in me not to love me.

With this in mind, I kept praying. Whenever I prayed with my heart focused on the Provider rather than on the provision, I felt better, more peaceful. But as soon as I shifted the focus to my needs I became anxious, caught up in trying to solve everything myself. I was like a hamster running furiously on a wheel while going nowhere.

But at least the anxiety was good for something. It was an alarm that told me I was heading in the wrong direction. I needed to pull my focus back toward God. Instead of thinking about all the things I couldn't do, I had to think about all the things he could do. Instead of thinking about my guilt, I had to think about his forgiveness. Instead of thinking of 1001 ways to solve my problems, I had to think about the countless ways God has already helped me in the past. And I had to keep reading the Scriptures, ones that spoke of God's intention to bless and provide.

Then things began to happen. First, I took a good hard look at my goals. What did I want for my family? What kind of financial plan might help us get there? My children needed to go to college, but I didn't want to have to work until I was ninety to pay for it. How did my spending habits need to change? Was there anything else in my attitude toward money that needed to change? These are important questions that my circumstances forced me to ask and keep asking.

Then, two days after I gave up looking for it, I found the permissions file.

Next, I discovered my financial situation was more positive than I had thought. Some important data had been left out of a report I had recently requested.

Then my accountant challenged a tax collection practice in my city and I received news of an unexpected refund for several years of overpayments.

Then, Kathy, the girls' nanny, and I talked about a way to restructure her job so that she could continue to be involved in our lives.

The process of learning to see God as my Provider continues. I am leaning on him more, withdrawing from him less. I am expecting him to take care of me even when I stumble, even when I don't fully understand or want to face the nature of my needs—like the need for repentance, correction, and trust. I realize that God's promised provision is conditional upon my obedience. But I also know that before I believed in him, Jesus provided for the greatest need of all—a way back to the Father who loves me. And he still provides a way back, even when I am tempted to think silly, childish thoughts about him.

Sunday

IN THE MORNING

I Will Not Forsake You

The LORD makes firm the steps
    of those who delight in him;
though they stumble, they will not fall,
    for the LORD upholds them with his hand.
I was young and now I am old,
    yet I have never seen the righteous forsaken
    or their children begging bread.
They are always generous and lend freely;
    their children will be a blessing.
Turn from evil and do good;
    then you will dwell in the land forever.
For the LORD loves the just
    and will not forsake his faithful ones.

Father, I have stumbled—many times. And just as many times you have kept me from falling. Thank you for your faithfulness. Help me to praise you by living a life in which you can delight.

Psalm 37:23–28 (TNIV)

AT NIGHT

I Will Throw Open the Floodgates of Heaven

"Bring the whole tithe into the storehouse, that there may be food in my house. Test me in this," says the LORD Almighty, "and see if I will not throw open the floodgates of heaven and pour out so much blessing that you will not have room enough for it. I will prevent pests from devouring your crops, and the vines in your fields will not cast their fruit," says the LORD Almighty. "Then all the nations will call you blessed, for yours will be a delightful land," says the LORD Almighty.

Lord, I want to take you at your word—to test your generosity by joyfully giving to others. Throw open the floodgates of heaven and open the gates of my heart. Let me give and give again as a way of celebrating your provision for me.

Malachi 3:10–12

155

Monday

IN THE MORNING

My Streams Are Filled with Water

You care for the land and water it;
    you enrich it abundantly.
The streams of God are filled with water
    to provide the people with grain,
    for so you have ordained it.
You drench its furrows
    and level its ridges;
you soften it with showers
    and bless its crops.
You crown the year with your bounty,
    and your carts overflow with abundance.
The grasslands of the desert overflow;
    the hills are clothed with gladness.
The meadows are covered with flocks
    and the valleys are mantled with grain;
    they shout for joy and sing.

Lord, you have made a bountiful world, capable of producing food, water, and shelter for everyone on the planet. Forgive us for hoarding its fruits and failing to care for it. Help us to learn one of the first lessons of childhood—to share what we have. May we become wise stewards, caring for the earth so that it can care for us.

Psalm 65:9–13

AT NIGHT

I Will Bless You Everywhere You Go

If you fully obey the LORD your God and carefully follow all his commands I give you today, the LORD your God will set you high above all the nations on earth. All these blessings will come upon you and accompany you if you obey the LORD your God:

You will be blessed in the city and blessed in the country.

The fruit of your womb will be blessed, and the crops of your land and the young of your livestock — the calves of your herds and the lambs of your flocks.

Your basket and your kneading trough will be blessed.

You will be blessed when you come in and blessed when you go out.

The LORD will grant that the enemies who rise up against you will be defeated before you. They will come at you from one direction but flee from you in seven.

The LORD will send a blessing on your barns and on everything you put your hand to. The LORD your God will bless you in the land he is giving you.

Lord, help me to learn from the story of your people. May obedience be the strong foundation on which my trust grows. Bless me in the city and in the country. Bless my children and my work. Bless me when I come in and when I go out. Let your blessings accompany me wherever I go.

Deuteronomy 28:1–8

Tuesday

IN THE MORNING

I Will Put You on Top, Not at the Bottom

May God give you of heaven's dew
  and of earth's richness —
  an abundance of grain and new wine.

The LORD will open the heavens, the storehouse of his bounty, to send rain on your land in season and to bless all the work of your hands. You will lend to many nations but will borrow from none. The LORD will make you the head, not the tail. If you pay attention to the commands of the LORD your God that I give you this day and carefully follow them, you will always be at the top, never at the bottom. Do not turn aside from any of the commands I give you today, to the right or to the left, following other gods and serving them.

Father, help me to appreciate the goodness of your commands. Make my obedience quick and full, not halting and partial. Give me the faith to follow regardless of what you ask. Open my eyes to your faithful provision.

Genesis 27:28; Deuteronomy 28:12 – 14

AT NIGHT

I Know About Your Hard Times

I will repay you for the years the locusts have eaten —
    the great locust and the young locust,
    the other locusts and the locust swarm —
    my great army that I sent among you.
You will have plenty to eat, until you are full,
    and you will praise the name of the LORD your God,
    who has worked wonders for you.

I will bless her with abundant provisions;
    her poor will I satisfy with food.

Lord, you have already performed wonders for me. You have seen the poverty of my soul and filled me with your presence. You have noted my hunger and given me a place at your table. You have blessed my family and cared for my children. Even in the hard times you have never left me. I praise your name, O faithful God!

Joel 2:25 – 26; Psalm 132:15

Wednesday

IN THE MORNING

You Will Be Like a Well-Watered Tree

The blessing of the LORD brings wealth,
    and he adds no trouble to it.

Blessed are those
    who do not walk in step with the wicked
or stand in the way that sinners take
    or sit in the company of mockers,
but who delight in the law of the LORD
    and meditate on his law day and night.
They are like a tree planted by streams of water,
    which yields its fruit in season
and whose leaf does not wither—
    whatever they do prospers.

Lord, let me be like a tree planted by streams of water, whose roots grow deep in you. No matter how parched the environment around me, nourish me with the life-giving water of your Spirit and your Word. May my life yield its fruit in due season.

Proverbs 10:22; Psalm 1:1–3 (TNIV)

AT NIGHT

I Am Your Provision

"The fire and wood are here," Isaac said, "but where is the lamb for the burnt offering?"

Abraham answered, "God himself will provide the lamb for the burnt offering, my son." And the two of them went on together....

Abraham looked up and there in a thicket he saw a ram caught by its horns. He went over and took the ram and sacrificed it as a burnt offering instead of his son. So Abraham called that place The LORD Will Provide. And to this day it is said, "On the mountain of the LORD it will be provided."

The next day John saw Jesus coming toward him and said, "Look, the Lamb of God, who takes away the sin of the world!"

Lord Jesus, more than all riches, I need the grace that flows because of your sacrificial offering on the cross. Thank you for being the Father's provision to make me whole.

Genesis 22:7–14; John 1:29

Thursday

IN THE MORNING

I Provide for All Who Grieve

The Spirit of the Sovereign LORD is on me,
   because the LORD has anointed me
   to preach good news to the poor.
He has sent me to bind up the brokenhearted,
   to proclaim freedom for the captives
   and release from darkness for the prisoners,
to proclaim the year of the LORD's favor
   and the day of vengeance of our God,
to comfort all who mourn,
   and provide for those who grieve in Zion—
to bestow on them a crown of beauty
   instead of ashes,
the oil of gladness
   instead of mourning,
and a garment of praise
   instead of a spirit of despair.
They will be called oaks of righteousness,
   a planting of the LORD.

Jesus, you came into my life as the greatest good news imaginable, healing my grief and giving me a future full of hope. You fill me with good things all the days of my life.

Isaiah 61:1–3

AT NIGHT

I Will Provide a Way Out

The LORD your God has blessed you in all the work of your hands. He has watched over your journey through this vast desert. These forty years the LORD your God has been with you, and you have not lacked anything.

So, if you think you are standing firm, be careful that you don't fall! No temptation has overtaken you except what is common to all. And God is faithful; he will not let you be tempted beyond what you can bear. But when you are tempted, he will also provide a way out so that you can endure it.

Lord, you know that life can sometimes be like a wilderness—dangerous, difficult, and lonely. And you know how discouraged I have sometimes been. Forgive my complaining and help me to remember that there is never a time when your grace is insufficient for my need.

Deuteronomy 2:7; 1 Corinthians 10:12–13 (TNIV)

January 1, 2016

Friday

IN THE MORNING

I Know What You Need

Who of you by worrying can add a single hour to his life? Since you cannot do this very little thing, why do you worry about the rest?

Consider how the lilies grow. They do not labor or spin. Yet I tell you, not even Solomon in all his splendor was dressed like one of these. If that is how God clothes the grass of the field, which is here today, and tomorrow is thrown into the fire, how much more will he clothe you, O you of little faith! And do not set your heart on what you will eat or drink; do not worry about it. For the pagan world runs after all such things, and your Father knows that you need them. But seek his kingdom, and these things will be given to you as well.

Lord, I need to relax—and to rest, to stop running so hard after the things of this world. Open my eyes to the ways you are providing for me right now. Give me the freedom of heart to spend myself on you.

Luke 12:25–31

AT NIGHT

Don't Let Fear Hold You Back

Do not be afraid, little flock, for your Father has been pleased to give you the kingdom. Sell your possessions and give to the poor. Provide purses for yourselves that will not wear out, a treasure in heaven that will not be exhausted, where no thief comes near and no moth destroys. For where your treasure is, there your heart will be also.

The generous will themselves be blessed,
    for they share their food with the poor.

Lord, increase my appetite for giving. Let nothing persuade me to withhold what you intend for others. May I open my hand freely, without fear, confident that you are more than able to provide for me as I provide for others.

Luke 12:32 – 34; Proverbs 22:9 (TNIV)

Saturday

IN THE MORNING

If You Ask, I Will Give

Ask and it will be given to you; seek and you will find; knock and the door will be opened to you. For everyone who asks receives; those who seek find; and to those who knock, the door will be opened.

Which of you, if his son asks for bread, will give him a stone? Or if he asks for a fish, will give him a snake? If you, then, though you are evil, know how to give good gifts to your children, how much more will your Father in heaven give good gifts to those who ask him!

Lord, I have asked—and you have given. I have knocked—and the door has been opened. Not once have you given me a stone when I asked for bread. Let the memory of your faithfulness encourage me to keep asking, seeking, and knocking, confident of your desire to bless and care for me.

Matthew 7:7–11 (TNIV)

AT NIGHT

Put Your Hope in Me

Command those who are rich in this present world not to be arrogant nor to put their hope in wealth, which is so uncertain, but to put their hope in God, who richly provides us with everything for our enjoyment. Command them to do good, to be rich in good deeds, and to be generous and willing to share. In this way they will lay up treasure for themselves as a firm foundation for the coming age, so that they may take hold of the life that is truly life.

Give, and it will be given to you. A good measure, pressed down, shaken together and running over, will be poured into your lap.

Father, help me to weigh and to value things as you do. Don't let the shining things of this world blind me to the beauty of your kingdom. Help me to reflect your abundant goodness by giving with a full heart to others.

1 Timothy 6:17–19; Luke 6:38

I WILL REMEMBER THIS

Ask and it will be given to you; seek and you will find; knock and the door will be opened to you.

Give, and it will be given to you. A good measure, pressed down, shaken together and running over, will be poured into your lap.

Who of you by worrying can add a single hour to his life? Since you cannot do this very little thing, why do you worry about the rest?

During the time I was worrying over my own set of problems, I saw on television how grief had etched itself into the faces of young African orphans with families decimated by AIDS, I read the story of three Christian men brutally murdered by Islamist extremists, and I heard through a school social worker about terrible difficulties facing a child in her care. My problems shrank to embarrassing insignificance. I realized that millions of suffering people throughout the world would gladly trade places with me if given the chance. It occurred to me they might even celebrate having the kind of problems that face a middle-class American like me.

I felt Christ nudging me to expand my circle of concern so that I could become part of his answer to the prayers of others.

Matthew 7:7; Luke 6:38; Luke 12:25–26

He wanted to remind me that his blessings are meant not just for me but for others. That I need to hold his gifts loosely so that I can become part of his answer to the prayers of others.

Last week I drove past another church and another sign. This one read: "Where God guides, he provides." There's certainly truth to this. But surely God's greatest provision is his mercy—and I have experienced so much mercy.

As I read and prayed about God's provision, I felt like so many tea leaves steeping in a pot, as though the Spirit of God was at work producing a rich brew whose healing properties were reshaping my distorted notions, increasing my gratitude, and giving me the faith to know that God cares for me regardless of appearances. When I think I need more money and God thinks I have enough. When I ask for better health and God allows me to be deprived of it. When my children have a problem and I don't know how to help them. When these things happen, I pray for the grace not to accuse God of forgetfulness and neglect but to call to mind his faithfulness, patiently awaiting his help.

9

God Speaks Words of Guidance

נָהַל

NAHAL

The Hebrew Scriptures speak of God as a shepherd carrying the lambs in his arms who gently leads (*nahal*) those that have young. Exodus portrays God as one who in his unfailing love will lead the people he has redeemed and who will guide (*nahal*) them in his strength. Though the Bible warns of snares, traps, and treacherous paths, it consistently portrays God as one who will counsel and safely guide all those who belong to him.

In the New Testament, the Greek word *hodos* refers to a path, road, street, or way, as in the statement in Matthew 7:13–14: "Enter through the narrow gate. For wide is the gate and broad is the *road* that leads to destruction, and many enter through it. But small is the gate and narrow the *road* that leads to life, and only a few find it." Jesus declares not only that he knows the way but that he is the way.

LETTING THE WORD SHAPE ME

A couple of years ago I traveled with friends to Greece. One of the strangest and most memorable days of our trip involved our ascent to the ruins of ancient Delphi, on the slopes of Mount Parnassus. According to legend, when Zeus released two eagles from the opposite sides of the earth, they flew round the world until they met in its exact center — Delphi.

Though settled in prehistoric times, most of the ruins at Delphi date back to the sixth century B.C. Here at the world's navel, the Greek god Apollo was said to have slaughtered a great serpent of the underworld — Python. As luck would have it, the snake's body tumbled into a fissure in the earth and began decaying, releasing fumes to the world above. The oracle, or prophetess, called Pythia, was an older woman of good repute who would stand over the opening allowing the vapor to envelop her. Intoxicated by the fumes, she would then utter cryptic prophecies to those who had made the arduous journey to Delphi for a glimpse of the future. To heighten the drama, she would then disappear, as if by magic. Close inspection of the ruins shows how she managed the trick, revealing a small tunnel through which a reasonably sized person could escape from the gullible crowd.

As bizarre as this ancient practice seems, it highlights how desperate humans have been through the ages for some kind of divine guidance. I remember a time in my own life when I was desperately seeking guidance for an important decision. Though I was never tempted to resort to divination, I do remember wishing God would make his answer so plain that I couldn't possibly mistake it. If only he would write it in the sky with big, bold, letters: ANN DO THIS! But God was more subtle — so subtle, in fact, that I didn't realize until years later that what mattered most was not what was written in the sky but what was written on my own heart.

In *The Will of God as a Way of Life,* Jerry Sittser examines the conventional approach to discovering God's will. According to this approach, every person in the world has a specific path to follow—a linear path that God alone knows. Like some Greek hero, we must, at every point, discover the only safe way ahead. After years of following this approach, Sittser began to perceive its flaws. For one thing, it provokes tremendous anxiety. Make a mistake and you miss your God-given destiny. For another, it overemphasizes the big decisions to the detriment of the small, character-shaping decisions we make every day, many of which have a far more profound influence on how our lives turn out (such as how we treat our spouses or children). For yet another, it assumes that God, who already seems to have great difficulty persuading us to do his will, would want to make things even harder by hiding that will from us.

I thought back to that time in my life when I had so anxiously been seeking God's guidance. If God had been tempted to write anything in the sky back then, it might have been this: ANN, RELAX! Since then, I have—at least when it comes to seeking God's guidance. The reason for my more relaxed approach is strictly experiential. I've found that as I've tried to do God's will, however imperfectly, God has guided me, not just once, but over and over. Now, as I read through words about guidance in the Scripture, they resonate not only with my mind but in my heart, because I have experienced them:

My Presence will go with you, and I will give you rest. (Exodus 33:14)

In your unfailing love you will lead the people you have redeemed. (Exodus 15:13)

I will turn the darkness into light before them and make the rough places smooth. (Isaiah 42:16)

Another reason for my more relaxed approach is that I think I can hear God more clearly than previously. Perhaps that's the way it should be. Instead of declining, as our physical senses do over time, our spiritual senses ought to become keener the longer we know God. As I thought about this, I began to wonder whether our ability to hear God's voice works something like memory foam. Like the warmth of our bodies giving shape to the foam, obedience gives shape to our hearts so that we can more readily receive impressions from God.

To say that I'm more relaxed isn't to say that I haven't made mistakes or that I won't in the future. But I trust that none of these will be fatal, that none will ultimately deflect me from the way God wants me to go. But guidance isn't really the hard part, as Jerry Sittser points out, for "if we sense any agony in the heroes of Scripture, it is not in discovering the will of God but in doing it." He goes on to say:

The will of God concerns the present more than the future ... The only time we really have both to know and to do God's will is the *present moment.* We are to love God with heart, soul, mind, and strength, and we are to love our neighbors as we love ourselves....

This perspective on the will of God gives us astonishing freedom. If we seek first God's kingdom and righteousness, which *is* the will of God for our lives, then *whatever choices we make concerning the future become the will of God for our lives.* There are many pathways we *could* follow, many options we *could* pursue. As long as we are seeking God, all of them can be God's will for our lives, although only one — the path we choose — actually becomes his will.

So today, when I am faced with a million little decisions, I pray for the grace to remember how simple it really is. Simple but not easy. For the way ahead will become clear as I practice the two great commandments — loving God with heart, mind, and strength, and loving my neighbor as myself.

Sunday

IN THE MORNING

I Will Go with You

Moses said to the LORD, "You have been telling me, 'Lead these people,' but you have not let me know whom you will send with me. You have said, 'I know you by name and you have found favor with me.' If you are pleased with me, teach me your ways so I may know you and continue to find favor with you. Remember that this nation is your people."

The LORD replied, "My Presence will go with you, and I will give you rest."

Then Moses said to him, "If your Presence does not go with us, do not send us up from here. How will anyone know that you are pleased with me and with your people unless you go with us? What else will distinguish me and your people from all the other people on the face of the earth?"

And the LORD said to Moses, "I will do the very thing you have asked, because I am pleased with you and I know you by name."

Lord, no path is good without your presence. In every decision, at every crossroad, help me to follow where you lead. Keep me from running ahead or lagging behind or wandering away, and let me know how near to me you are.

Exodus 33:12–17

AT NIGHT

I Will Make a Way

Then the angel of God, who had been traveling in front of Israel's army, withdrew and went behind them. The pillar of cloud also moved from in front and stood behind them, coming between the armies of Egypt and Israel. Throughout the night the cloud brought darkness to the one side and light to the other side; so neither went near the other all night long.

Then Moses stretched out his hand over the sea, and all that night the LORD drove the sea back with a strong east wind and turned it into dry land. The waters were divided, and the Israelites went through the sea on dry ground, with a wall of water on their right and on their left.

Lord, thank you for guiding me across difficult terrain at various points in my life, opening a way when all ways seemed closed. I marvel at who you are—the almighty God who is able to confuse the plans of those who oppose you and enlighten the way of those who love you. I love you, Lord.

Exodus 14:19–22

Monday

IN THE MORNING

My Spirit Will Guide You

Because of your great compassion you did not abandon them in the desert. By day the pillar of cloud did not cease to guide them on their path, nor the pillar of fire by night to shine on the way they were to take. You gave your good Spirit to instruct them. You did not withhold your manna from their mouths, and you gave them water for their thirst. For forty years you sustained them in the desert; they lacked nothing, their clothes did not wear out nor did their feet become swollen.

> In your unfailing love you will lead
> the people you have redeemed.
> In your strength you will guide them
> to your holy dwelling.

Father, help me to remember that I'm not alone on this journey. Let me look for the guidance of your good Spirit, believing that you will not withhold the things I need even when life feels like a wilderness. Help me to rely on your love and trust in your mercy.

Nehemiah 9:19–21; Exodus 15:13

AT NIGHT

I Won't Let You Lose Your Way

I will lead the blind by ways they have not known,
    along unfamiliar paths I will guide them;
I will turn the darkness into light before them
    and make the rough places smooth.
These are the things I will do;
    I will not forsake them.

They will neither hunger nor thirst,
    nor will the desert heat or the sun beat upon them.
He who has compassion on them will guide them
    and lead them beside springs of water.
I will turn all my mountains into roads,
    and my highways will be raised up.

Lord, it doesn't matter how well I see but how well you see. Help me to trust your vision for the way ahead. And as we walk it together, smooth out my path, not so that everything is easy, but so that everything is possible.

Isaiah 42:16; Isaiah 49:10–11

Tuesday

IN THE MORNING

I Will Lead You on a Safe Path

When Pharaoh let the people go, God did not lead them on the road through the Philistine country, though that was shorter. For God said, "If they face war, they might change their minds and return to Egypt." So God led the people around by the desert road toward the Red Sea. The Israelites went up out of Egypt armed for battle.

You broaden the path beneath me,
so that my ankles do not turn.

Lord, it's easy to pray as though I know where I'm going, as though you simply need to come alongside and bless my plans. Forgive me. Today, I pray for the grace to want to be led. When the way ahead seems tortuously long or slow, help me to trust that you know where we are going — and why.

Exodus 13:17 – 18; 2 Samuel 22:37

AT NIGHT

I Will Guide You Always

The LORD will guide you always.

Where can I go from your Spirit?
    Where can I flee from your presence?
If I go up to the heavens, you are there;
    if I make my bed in the depths, you are there.
If I rise on the wings of the dawn,
    if I settle on the far side of the sea,
even there your hand will guide me,
    your right hand will hold me fast.

Father, thank you for your promise, that even in the darkness I will not be left alone, without direction. Instead of panicking or plunging ahead blindly when I feel perplexed or confused, uncertain of the way ahead, help me to listen and to wait patiently for you to guide me.

Isaiah 58:11; Psalm 139:7–10

Wednesday

IN THE MORNING

I Will Lead You into a Good Land

The path of the righteous is level;
> O upright One, you make the way of the righteous
> smooth.
Yes, Lord, walking in the way of your laws,
> we wait for you;
your name and renown
> are the desire of our hearts.

Observe the commands of the Lord your God, walking in his ways and revering him. For the Lord your God is bringing you into a good land—a land with streams and pools of water, with springs flowing in the valleys and hills; a land with wheat and barley, vines and fig trees, pomegranates, olive oil and honey; a land where bread will not be scarce and you will lack nothing.

Father, let me take pleasure in pleasing you. Change my reluctant obedience into something quick and strong. Give me joy as you lead me into the good land you have promised.

Isaiah 26:7–8; Deuteronomy 8:6–9

AT NIGHT

I Will Counsel You

I will instruct you and teach you in the way you should go;
    I will counsel you with my loving eye on you.
Do not be like the horse or the mule,
    which have no understanding
but must be controlled by bit and bridle
    or they will not come to you.
Many are the woes of the wicked,
    but the LORD's unfailing love
surrounds those who trust in him.

The LORD makes firm the steps
    of those who delight in him;
Though they stumble, they will not fall,
    for the LORD upholds them with his hand.

Lord, help me to believe that your loving eye really is on me. Free me from the fear that your way is too hard. Make me less obstinate and more malleable, trusting that your ways are good.

Psalm 32:8–10 (TNIV); Psalm 37:23–24 (TNIV)

Thursday

IN THE MORNING

I Will Guide You into All Truth

The path of the righteous is like the first gleam of dawn,
   shining ever brighter till the full light of day.

I have much more to say to you, more than you can now bear.
But when he, the Spirit of truth, comes, he will guide you into all
truth. He will not speak on his own; he will speak only what he
hears, and he will tell you what is yet to come. He will bring glory
to me by taking from what is mine and making it known to you.
All that belongs to the Father is mine. That is why I said the Spirit
will take from what is mine and make it known to you.

*Lord, you are the light of the world, the shining One whose glory
I want to reflect. Let your truth guide me and lead me. Send your
Spirit that I may know your ways.*

Proverbs 4:18; John 16:12–15

AT NIGHT

My Commands Will Be a Light for Your Path

My son, keep your father's commands
    and do not forsake your mother's teaching.
Bind them upon your heart forever;
    fasten them around your neck
When you walk, they will guide you;
    when you sleep, they will watch over you;
    when you awake, they will speak to you.
For these commands are a lamp,
    this teaching is a light,
and the corrections of discipline
    are the way to life.

Lord, help me to think of your commands not as a burden but as a beam of light, shining on the path ahead. Wherever I walk let them guide me.

Proverbs 6:20–23

Friday

IN THE MORNING

I Have the Understanding You Need

This is what the LORD says:

"Stand at the crossroads and look;
    ask for the ancient paths,
ask where the good way is, and walk in it,
    and you will find rest for your souls."

Counsel and sound judgment are mine;
    I have understanding and power....
I love those who love me,
    and those who seek me find me.

Lord, you do understand—everything. You know what has happened, what is happening, and what will happen. You know me. Guide me today with your counsel. Teach me to make every decision with the help of your Spirit.

Jeremiah 6:16; Proverbs 8:14, 17

AT NIGHT

I Am the Way

Jesus answered, "I am the way and the truth and the life. No one comes to the Father except through me. If you really knew me, you would know my Father as well. From now on, you do know him and have seen him."

I am the vine; you are the branches. If you remain in me and I in you, you will bear much fruit; apart from me you can do nothing.... If you remain in me and my words remain in you, ask whatever you wish, and it will be done for you. This is to my Father's glory, that you bear much fruit, showing yourselves to be my disciples.

Lord, the way ahead isn't always as complicated as I make it, for you are the way. As long as I stay connected to you, I will fulfill your purpose for my life. Help me, Lord, to abide in you.

John 14:6–7; John 15:5–8 (TNIV)

Saturday

IN THE MORNING

I Will Be Your Guide Even to the End

Search me, O God, and know my heart;
 test me and know my anxious thoughts.
See if there is any offensive way in me,
 and lead me in the way everlasting.

For this God is our God for ever and ever;
 he will be our guide even to the end.

Father, thank you for your promise to be with me to the end—to the last day, the last moment, the last breath. With this knowledge, let fear fade and hope grow strong. For you are my God forever, and you will be my guide even to the end.

Psalm 139:23–24; Psalm 48:14

AT NIGHT

I Will Lead You Home

Yet I am always with you;
    you hold me by my right hand.
You guide me with your counsel,
    and afterward you will take me into glory.
Whom have I in heaven but you?
    And earth has nothing I desire besides you.
My flesh and my heart may fail,
    but God is the strength of my heart
    and my portion forever.

Lord, you know better than I how weak I am — how prone to falling. Yet you hold onto me through the long years and the difficult days, through the joys and the celebrations, through the decisions and the opportunities. In my weakness you strengthen me, leading me home, guiding me with your counsel, keeping me safe.

Psalm 73:23–26

I WILL REMEMBER THIS

The LORD replied, "My Presence will go with you, and I will give you rest."

———

In your unfailing love you will lead
    the people you have redeemed.

———

The LORD will guide you always.

———

Stand at the crossroads and look;
    ask for the ancient paths,
ask where the good way is, and walk in it,
    and you will find rest for your souls.

So many of the Bible's great stories are about movement and journey. Adam and Eve are ejected from paradise; Abraham and Sarah are called to move to a strange, new land; Jacob and his sons travel to Egypt to escape a famine; Moses leads the Israelites out of Egypt; Joshua leads them into the Promised Land; Jonah runs away from God and God runs after him; Paul is converted on the road to Damascus. Even Jesus journeys up to Jerusalem to meet his destiny, and then he leaves the earth to ascend to heaven. No wonder Scripture seems always to be

Exodus 33:14; Exodus 15:13; Isaiah 58:11; Jeremiah 6:16

talking about the *path* or the *way*. God's people are always going somewhere.

Like them, it occurs to me that I am also on the move because the life of faith always leads somewhere. Why, then, would I ever approach a decision in isolation, as though my life is made up of a series of random happenings leading nowhere in particular? Why, for instance, would I consider a job change merely on the merits of how it might affect my bank statement or my ego? Why would I date someone who isn't traveling the path I am? Why would I allow myself to become so busy that I forget whether I'm coming or going?

I've always been interested in interior design, but it's a profession I could never excel at. Though I love beautiful objects, I have a hard time envisioning how everything will fit together — how a home will look once the walls are painted, draperies are hung, rugs are laid, and furniture is selected and arranged. No wonder I've sometimes found myself with a collection of attractive items that simply don't fit in any room of the house.

But how does my problem with interior design connect to decision-making and the need for guidance? Simply that with every significant choice, there's a bigger picture to keep in mind. Though I don't have the complete picture, God does.

From the very beginning of my journey with Christ, I am called to have faith and then to keep faith at every point along the way, remembering that God has promised to guide me all the way through to the end — even to the bitter end when I am surrounded by weakness, illness, suffering, and death. Yes, as the psalmist declares, even when I walk though the valley of the shadow of death, I will fear no evil, for the Lord's goodness and kindness will follow me and I will dwell in his house forever.

10

God Speaks Word of Faithfulness

אֱמוּנָה אָמַן

EMUNAH, AMAN

Faithfulness is an essential characteristic of God. He wouldn't be God without it. Because he is faithful, we can lean on him, count on him, and believe in him. It's what makes obedience not only possible but prudent. In fact, God's faithfulness is meant to call out the same quality in those who believe in him.

In Greek the word for "faithful" is *pistos*, as in 1 Corinthians 10:13: "And God is faithful; he will not let you be tempted beyond what you can bear." God's faithfulness is what enables us to say "amen," a word that derives directly from the Hebrew word *aman*.

As believers we are called to be faithful to Christ even under the threat of death. For most of us, faithfulness is a far more ordinary virtue, consisting as it does, not in a single heroic act but in daily obedience, in the decision to trust in God's goodness and believe in his promises. Unbelief is fueled by fear, pride, self-reliance, and self-seeking. To be faithless is to be out of step and out of sync with God. To be faithful is to align ourselves with God, acknowledging him as mighty, good, and loving toward all he has made.

LETTING THE WORD SHAPE ME

I realize there are some advantages to being married. For one, you can blame your spouse whenever something goes wrong. As a single mother, I don't have that luxury. But a few years ago I still managed to find someone to blame when one of my children was suffering through a rough patch. I'll give you a clue. His name starts with a "G" and ends with a "d." It is composed of three letters, the middle one of which is "o." Yes, I blamed God, and I blamed him big time.

Why wasn't he helping my child? Hadn't he handpicked her for our family when I adopted her? Didn't he know what she was going through? Didn't he hear the prayers that family and friends had raised so constantly on her behalf? I had literally cried out to him more than once, begging for his help. But all I heard was silence—a big nothing. Didn't he know I was at my limit, that I was about to blow up with the stress I felt because of my inability to help my child? Why did he refuse to help?

When my daughter was young she suffered from acute anxiety, which made her over-reactive to situations that most children take in stride. I felt bad for her and for me. So bad in fact that I began accusing God—he wasn't listening, wasn't acting, wasn't living up to all the good press he has gotten. I was angry and as close to despair as I had ever come, so close in fact that it shocked me.

So I did the only thing I could think of—I confided in a few close friends, women with whom I gather regularly for mutual support and prayer. I told them exactly how I was feeling. In an instant, they encircled me, laying their hands gently on my shoulder, asking God to help my daughter and me. After a moment or two, one of them said she felt the hair on her neck prickling, standing straight up — she could literally feel the presence of evil in the room. So she led the others in praying against it as they surrounded me with their love and concern. Immediately my despair lifted, and it has never returned.

Soon after that prayer session with friends, everything seemed to come together for my daughter and me. A friend and her husband invited her to spend time with them, giving us a much-needed break. Then my daughter began to calm down. She was happy, curious, affectionate, and funny again — the little girl I remembered. In fact, she was doing better than she ever had. Our relationship, which had been in such bad repair, was flourishing. We were happy together. It soon became clear that her new medicine was working after weeks of a difficult transition.

Now, some years later, as I read and meditate on passages concerning God's faithfulness, I remember that time — perhaps because God's faithfulness stands so vividly in contrast to my own faithlessness, like a brilliant white diamond resting on a black velvet background. Since then, I have come to appreciate Jim Cymbala's observation about how difficult it can be to wait on God for answers to our prayers.

> It is during the waiting that discouragement often sets in. It is also the time when Satan slanders God and puts powerful temptations before us ... The glow of fresh faith fades away as the days, weeks, months, and sometimes even years go by without seeing our prayers answered. *Will things ever change?* We wonder. *Is it worth it to keep on trying to believe? ...* The challenge before us is to have faith in God, and the hardest part of faith is the *waiting.* And the hardest part of waiting is the last half hour.

It was that last half hour that nearly did me in. As I think back to that time, I also recall a promise from Isaiah quoted in Matthew's gospel: "A bruised reed he will not break, and a smoldering wick he will not snuff out" (Matthew 12:20). I had felt like such a "bruised reed of a mother," so unable to cope with my daughter's affliction. And yet God had not snuffed out my smoldering faith but had succeeded in sparking it again. Despite my feelings to the contrary, he had seen our need, heard our prayers, and was in the process of answering them.

I realize now how dangerous my anger was. It had led me into making false accusations against God, bringing me to the edge of despair. I know that some people think it's all right to get angry with God. He can take it, they say. But the problem is that I can't take it. My anger distorts reality, making God into someone he's not — someone distant and absent, someone powerful but uncaring.

Since that difficult time in our family, I've concluded that it is okay for me to get angry *in* God's presence but that I can never allow myself to get angry *at* God. I can be completely honest with him about how I am feeling, but I can't afford to project my anger onto him, contradicting what he has already revealed about himself in Scripture and in his dealings with me.

It occurs to me that faith involves buying into a story—an overarching narrative that makes sense out of the universe and our part in it. The hero of the Christian narrative, of course, is God, who begins by creating us and who then draws his wayward people back to himself in the most costly way imaginable. Our relationship with the Hero is what gives us purpose, dignity, and hope. Even so, we sometimes forget essential elements of the story. When this happens, another narrative emerges, one that is distorted, disheartening, and confusing. We find ourselves questioning what we once believed. Is the Hero who we thought he was? Will he keep his promises? If so, why does he seem so silent, so hidden? Does he really love us?

Last week a friend lost his job. I imagined myself in his place. How tough it must have been to be abruptly cut loose from an organization you have served so long and well. When I conveyed my dismay at the news, he wrote back: "I am confident that God owns the narrative and that these unwelcome times are in his capable hands." I loved his response. While honestly characterizing the situation as "unwelcome," he came to a stunning conclusion: "God owns the narrative!" Grasping that is the key to remaining faithful to God no matter what.

Thank God that there is nothing fickle or faithless about him. With St. Paul who proclaimed Christ from a Roman dungeon, shortly before his death, I stand as a witness to the truth that even "if we are faithless, he will remain faithful, for he cannot disown himself" (2 Timothy 2:13).

God help me to remain faithful in the days ahead.

Sunday

IN THE MORNING

I Have Promised to Love You

The LORD did not set his affection on you and choose you because you were more numerous than other peoples, for you were the fewest of all peoples. But it was because the LORD loved you and kept the oath he swore to your forefathers that he brought you out with a mighty hand and redeemed you from the land of slavery, from the power of Pharaoh king of Egypt. Know therefore that the LORD your God is God; he is the faithful God, keeping his covenant of love to a thousand generations of those who love him and keep his commands.

God, who has called you into fellowship with his Son Jesus Christ our Lord, is faithful.

Lord, thank you for setting your affection on me, never wavering in your kindness. Help me to remember the countless ways you have already shown your love—to your people and to me. Let me proclaim your goodness so that others will know who you are.

Deuteronomy 7:7–9; 1 Corinthians 1:9

AT NIGHT

I Am Faithful Even When You Are Unfaithful

So Moses chiseled out two stone tablets like the first ones and went up Mount Sinai early in the morning, as the LORD had commanded him; and he carried the two stone tablets in his hands. Then the LORD came down in the cloud and stood there with him and proclaimed his name, the LORD. And he passed in front of Moses, proclaiming, "The LORD, the LORD, the compassionate and gracious God, slow to anger, abounding in love and faithfulness, maintaining love to thousands, and forgiving wickedness, rebellion and sin.

Lord, I am amazed at the way you describe yourself. Instead of choosing words like powerful, awesome, terrible, or great, you use words like compassion, love, and faithfulness. Even more amazing — this revelation occurred right after your people had been unfaithful — worshiping a golden calf. Thank you for never abandoning them or me — for the gift of your forgiveness and your patience.

Exodus 34:4–6

Monday

IN THE MORNING

I Am Faithful in Every Way

For the word of the LORD is right and true;
>   he is faithful in all he does.
The LORD loves righteousness and justice;
>   the earth is full of his unfailing love.

Your love, LORD, reaches to the heavens,
>   your faithfulness to the skies.
Your righteousness is like the highest mountains,
>   your justice like the great deep.
>   You, LORD, preserve both people and animals.
How priceless is your unfailing love, O God!
>   People take refuge in the shadow of your wings.
They feast on the abundance of your house;
>   you give them drink from your river of delights.
For with you is the fountain of life;
>   in your light we see light.

Father, your goodness is unfathomable — too high, too deep, too wide for me. Open my eyes to the way the whole earth is full of your unfailing love.

Psalm 33:4–5; Psalm 36:5–9 (TNIV)

AT NIGHT

I Love What I've Made

The LORD is faithful to all his promises
    and loving toward all he has made.
The LORD upholds all those who fall
    and lifts up all who are bowed down.
The eyes of all look to you,
    and you give them their food at the proper time.
You open your hand
    and satisfy the desires of every living thing.
The LORD is righteous in all his ways
    and loving toward all he has made.
The LORD is near to all who call on him,
    to all who call on him in truth.
He fulfills the desires of those who fear him;
    he hears their cry and saves them.
The LORD watches over all who love him.

You, Lord, are loving toward all you have made. That means your intentions toward every human being, every animal, every leaf and twig are always and everywhere good. Help me to stand on that loving foundation. May your great faithfulness shape my thoughts and govern my actions, now and always. Amen.

Psalm 145:13–20

Tuesday

IN THE MORNING

You Can Trust Me

Trust in him at all times, O people;
    pour out your hearts to him,
    for God is our refuge.

I will proclaim the name of the LORD.
    Oh, praise the greatness of our God!
He is the Rock, his works are perfect,
    and all his ways are just.
A faithful God who does no wrong,
    upright and just is he.

Father, I've lived long enough to know that no human being is entirely trustworthy—including me. But you are not like us, saying one thing and then doing another. Help me to trust you enough to be honest about my failings and confident enough about your response. Help me to wait patiently and confidently for your help.

Psalm 62:8; Deuteronomy 32:3–4

AT NIGHT

I Will Give What Is Good

I will listen to what God the LORD will say;
>   he promises peace to his people, his saints—
>   but let them not return to folly.
Surely his salvation is near those who fear him,
>   that his glory may dwell in our land.
Love and faithfulness meet together;
>   righteousness and peace kiss each other.
Faithfulness springs forth from the earth,
>   and righteousness looks down from heaven.
The LORD will indeed give what is good,
>   and our land will yield its harvest.

Father, send your love and your faithfulness to help me. Enable me to respond to you with faithful obedience, creating an opportunity for your perfect will to be done on this earth. May my life yield its harvest, according to your purpose, I pray.

Psalm 85:8–12

Wednesday

IN THE MORNING

You Can Put Your Hope in the Words I Have Spoken

Praise the LORD, all you nations;
  extol him, all you peoples.
For great is his love toward us,
  and the faithfulness of the LORD endures forever.

May those who fear you rejoice when they see me,
  for I have put my hope in your word.
I know, O LORD, that your laws are righteous,
  and in faithfulness you have afflicted me.
May your unfailing love be my comfort,
  according to your promise to your servant.
Let your compassion come to me that I may live,
  for your law is my delight.

Lord, let me trust you even when I am afflicted. May nothing defeat my belief in your goodness. When I feel confused and overwhelmed, show me your compassion. Use the hard things to bring good things to me and to others.

Psalm 117:1–2; Psalm 119:74–77

AT NIGHT

My Love Preserves You

I remember my affliction and my wandering,
>   the bitterness and the gall.
I well remember them,
>   and my soul is downcast within me.
Yet this I call to mind
>   and therefore I have hope:
Because of the LORD's great love we are not consumed,
>   for his compassions never fail.
They are new every morning;
>   great is your faithfulness.

Lord, in the midst of great sorrow—even then you comfort me. Help me to call to mind your great faithfulness, the kindness you have already shown. Never let me despair of your help. Instead let me look for your mercy, for it is new every morning.

Lamentations 3:19–23

Thursday

IN THE MORNING

I Am Faithful Forever

The Lord is faithful, and he will strengthen and protect you from the evil one.

May God himself, the God of peace, sanctify you through and through. May your whole spirit, soul and body be kept blameless at the coming of our Lord Jesus Christ. The one who calls you is faithful and he will do it.

I saw heaven standing open and there before me was a white horse, whose rider is called Faithful and True.

Lord, as I look back over my life I cannot identify a single moment in which you have ever failed me or proven faithless. Your care has been constant even when I couldn't see it. I would be foolish not to trust you. No matter what happens, I know the One who has called me is faithful and he will do it!

2 Thessalonians 3:3; 1 Thessalonians 5:23–24; Revelation 19:11

AT NIGHT

I Keep Every Promise

But as surely as God is faithful, our message to you is not "Yes" and "No." For the Son of God, Jesus Christ, who was preached among you by me and Silas and Timothy, was not "Yes" and "No," but in him it has always been "Yes." For no matter how many promises God has made, they are "Yes" in Christ. And so through him the "Amen" is spoken by us to the glory of God. Now it is God who makes both us and you stand firm in Christ. He anointed us, set his seal of ownership on us, and put his Spirit in our hearts as a deposit, guaranteeing what is to come.

Lord, I can stand firm because you stand firm. I can remain faithful because you've given your Son to save me and your Spirit to guide me. Thank you for not wavering in your plan, for not forgetting your promises. Help me to wait confidently for every one of them to come true.

2 Corinthian 1:18–22

Friday

IN THE MORNING

Believe in Me

Here is a trustworthy saying:

If we died with him,
   we will also live with him;
if we endure,
   we will also reign with him.
If we disown him,
   he will also disown us;
if we are faithless,
   he will remain faithful,
      for he cannot disown himself.

Then they asked him, "What must we do to do the works God requires?"

Jesus answered, "The work of God is this: to believe in the one he has sent."

Lord, my faith has not always been unwavering. Yet you have never failed me. Today I pray that you will give me what I need most — more staying power, more zeal, more courage, and more love. Through my life, may you proclaim your great faithfulness.

2 Timothy 2:11 – 13; John 6:28 – 29

AT NIGHT

My Eyes Are on the Faithful

My eyes will be on the faithful in the land,
that they may dwell with me.

And God is faithful; he will not let you be tempted beyond what you can bear. But when you are tempted, he will also provide a way out so that you can stand up under it.

Be faithful, even to the point of death, and I will give you the crown of life.

Lord, sometimes it feels as though you're asking the impossible. Yet, I've found that your grace enables me to do what I cannot possibly do on my own. Help me to stand faithfully in the midst of trials, waiting confidently for your deliverance.

Psalm 101:6; 1 Corinthians 10:13; Revelation 2:10

Saturday

IN THE MORNING

I Can Do Great Things with Your Life

By faith Abraham, when called to go to a place he would later receive as his inheritance, obeyed and went, even though he did not know where he was going. By faith he made his home in the promised land like a stranger in a foreign country....

By faith Abraham, even though he was past age—and Sarah herself was barren—was enabled to become a father because he considered him faithful who had made the promise. And so from this one man, and he as good as dead, came descendants as numerous as the stars in the sky and as countless as the sand on the seashore.

Lord, I want you to use my life in the greatest way possible, not so that I can get glory but so that you can. Increase my faith, stretch it, make it strong. May faith be the hallmark of my life. Accomplish your purpose through me.

Hebrews 11:8–9, 11–12

AT NIGHT

Do Not Rely on Yourself

But the fruit of the Spirit is love, joy, peace, patience, kindness, goodness, faithfulness, gentleness and self-control. Against such things there is no law.

My son, do not forget my teaching,
    but keep my commands in your heart,
for they will prolong your life many years
    and bring you prosperity.
Let love and faithfulness never leave you;
    bind them around your neck,
    write them on the tablet of your heart....
Trust in the LORD with all your heart
    and lean not on your own understanding....
Do not be wise in your own eyes;
    fear the LORD and shun evil.
This will bring health to your body
    and nourishment to your bones.

Lord, with your help I will trust you with all my heart, never doubting your intentions or misconstruing your motives. I will keep your love and faithfulness in the forefront of my mind so that no circumstance in my life will be untouched by your love.

Galatians 5:22–23; Proverbs 3:1–3, 5, 7–8

I WILL REMEMBER THIS

The LORD is faithful to all his promises
    and loving toward all he has made.
The LORD upholds all those who fall
    and lifts up all who are bowed down.

Because of the LORD's great love we are not consumed,
    for his compassions never fail.
They are new every morning;
    great is your faithfulness.

Let love and faithfulness never leave you;
    bind them around your neck,
    write them on the tablet of your heart....
Trust in the LORD with all your heart
    and lean not on your own understanding.

Mark Buchanan is a personal friend, a client, and one of my favorite authors. Over lunch one day, he tossed out a phrase to describe a book he was thinking about writing. He spoke about the need for "resting in the character of God." I love that phrase because it captures the essence of faithfulness.

Whenever my faith has been shaken, it has inevitably been when I have tried "resting in circumstances" rather than "resting in the character of God." Something in my brain keeps

Psalm 145:13–14; Lamentations 3:22–23; Proverbs 3:3, 5

advancing the "if only lie." "*If only* I had more energy; *if only* I had more time; *if only* my children would ..." Even in good times, I can always come up with another *if only*. But Jesus doesn't promise to rearrange our circumstances, to smooth everything out for us. That's not what we put our faith in. In fact Jesus once remarked that *each day has enough trouble of its own.*

Resting in our circumstances, then, is like trying to relax on a bed of nails or on the deck of a ship that is being tossed about on a roiling ocean. A sudden surge and we're likely to be pitched overboard. We know that circumstances can change in an instant. The only thing that will never change is God's character, his intentions, his heart. That's the stable foundation in which we can rest.

But what does that mean practically speaking? At the least it means that I have to act as though I believe God is faithful, as though his intentions toward me are always good and never evil. I put my faith in him. I act with faithfulness toward him, obeying his commands, yielding to his guidance.

The letter to the Hebrews tells us that "without faith it is impossible to please God" (Hebrews 11:6). That's a simple statement of fact, like saying that without air it's impossible to breathe, without food you can't survive, or when your eyes are closed you can't see. Faith opens our eyes to the goodness and trustworthiness of God. We live by faith and not by sight. There is no other way, no other promise, no other strategy that will yield the life we desire, the life we were meant to live.

11

God Speaks Words of Hope and Comfort

יָחַל תִּקְוָה נָחַם

YAHAL, TIQWA, NAHAM

ope (*yahal* and *tiqwa*), in the biblical sense, has little to do with wishful thinking and everything to do with confident expectation. Hope is rooted not in circumstances but in God himself. Hope has been described as an anchor for our souls because it is grounded in the unchanging nature and intentions of God. Hope steadies our hearts by enabling us to wait confidently for what we desire most—the joy of living in God's presence.

The Hebrew word *naham* can be translated "to comfort" or "to console." God is the ultimate source of comfort, the only one capable of turning our desolation to joy. Metaphors of God as a shepherd or as a mother describe his comfort in a particularly poignant way.

The New Testament makes it clear that God is the source of all comfort. In fact, the King James Version of the Bible calls the Holy Spirit "the Comforter." Jesus, too, spoke of his desire to comfort his people, yearning to gather them to himself as a hen gathers her chicks under his wings. Ultimately, God comforts us by sending his Son to save us, releasing us from sin's bondage and destining us for a future full of hope.

LETTING THE WORD SHAPE ME

It's the day after Thanksgiving. Yesterday at this time, our house was spilling over with the rich smells of a harvest feast. It was full of people laughing and dogs barking. A fire was roaring in the hearth. We even had three birthdays to celebrate so there were cards and presents, a cake with candles, and a little off-key singing to mark the occasion.

Today is different—not only quieter but a little somber. It's not that I'm suffering from post-holiday depression. It's that I've been thinking about my Christmas card list, realizing how difficult this year has been for some. In fact, if you wanted a microcosm of many common kinds of loss, you need only look at my list: one person died, one suffered a fall from grace, one was seriously ill, one lost his job, and two divorced. And these were merely the obvious losses—the kind people can't easily hide. What, I wondered, about the private grief people silently harbor? Aren't most of us in need of some kind of comfort and enduring hope?

I thought, too, about the limits of comfort, at least the human variety. In the face of tragedy it can be difficult to know how to console someone. We don't have the resources to do what we would like to—reverse a financial loss, heal the sick, restore a reputation, or mend broken relationships. Our unease in the face of loss can be so extreme that at times it provokes us into making idiotic comments, like the one I once heard at a funeral when one of the guests remarked that the flowers draping the casket were so beautiful they almost looked artificial! Or like the woman I overheard trying to console a bereaved husband by assuring him that his wife looked more beautiful lying in her coffin than she ever had when she was alive.

But worse than blurting out insensitive comments in our attempt to fill the awkward silence is the insensitivity of not showing up at all. Recently, one of my mother's closest friends became an invalid, confined to her bed in a nursing home. She, too, is on my Christmas list. Though I had prayed for her regularly, I remember how I responded when my mother suggested I visit her. I felt put out, as if she was asking too much. Didn't she know I was busy? That I had a book to write, clients to help, children to care for?

But as soon as I spoke my complaint, I felt ashamed. How could I reduce another person's suffering to a mere inconvenience? Did everything revolve around my needs, my concerns, my schedule? What if I were lying in that bed? I felt repulsed by what my response had revealed about the condition of my heart. For the good of my soul I knew I needed to offer the small gift of my presence to a woman who had been a family friend for many years. So I went and felt comforted by the gift of her presence, lying as she did in that bed with so much patience and good nature.

One of the most popular passages in the Bible is Psalm 23. It's a comfort to the living as well as to those near death.

Even though I walk
    through the valley of the shadow of death,
I will fear no evil,
    for you are with me;
your rod and your staff,
    they comfort me.

God is the Shepherd who will not fail to show up when we need him. He is strong and loving enough to help us pass safely through death's shadow. Isn't that the ultimate comfort—to believe that because we belong to God the end will be sweet and not bitter, that heaven awaits us even in the midst of whatever hellishness we suffer?

Last night I asked a couple of friends whether they ever doubted the existence of an afterlife. One admitted she had doubts at times but said she had also had experiences of the supernatural that convinced her there was something beyond this life. Then my friend Patti related an experience she had a few years ago.

Alone at home one night, Patti had been reading the newspaper when the music began. It was exquisite—strange but beautiful. Certain the music wasn't coming from a television, radio, or DVD player, Patti walked through the house trying to locate the source. But a thorough search revealed nothing. Then she opened the front door, but all was quiet. That was when she realized the music was coming from inside. Patti was hearing the music inside her head. Her first thought was to wonder whether she might be losing her mind. But what a pleasant way to go! Then, after about thirty minutes, the music stopped.

Shortly after that Patti heard a siren and noticed the flashing red light of an ambulance as it pulled into the driveway next door. Though her neighbors hadn't lived there long, Patti knew the wife had been suffering from Lou Gehrig's disease. She watched as paramedics carried her out on a stretcher.

The woman's suffering, she learned, had ended that night. At the exact time Patti had been hearing the music, it seems that her neighbor had been passing from this life to the next. Later she told the woman's husband she was certain she had heard the voices of angels rejoicing, singing as they carried his wife to heaven.

Psalm 116 assures us that God knows the exact time of our passing. He will not be preoccupied, looking the other way when it's time for us to go. In fact, the contrary is true as the psalmist says, for "precious in the sight of the LORD is the death of his saints" (Psalm 116:15). Jesus made a similar point by noting that not even a sparrow falls to the ground without the Father knowing it.

Ultimately, it would seem that our best hope of comfort resides in the presence of God himself: in his faithfulness, his kindness, his unchanging nature, his ability to keep his promises. To paraphrase Paul, nothing can separate us from the love of Christ, not job loss, family trouble, loneliness, misunderstanding, failure, or even Lou Gehrig's disease. Our bodies may betray us, our families forsake us, our friends fail us, but the all-important truth is that if God is for us, then nothing can defeat us.

Sunday

IN THE MORNING

I Am One Who Comforts You

I, even I, am he who comforts you.

"For I know the plans I have for you," declares the LORD, "plans to prosper you and not to harm you, plans to give you hope and a future. Then you will call upon me and come and pray to me, and I will listen to you. You will seek me and find me when you seek me with all your heart. I will be found by you," declares the LORD.

Lord, when every other comfort fails, you are still with us. Give us the grace—today, tomorrow, and the next day—to set aside our doubting thoughts. Help us, in the midst of sorrow, to sense your presence. Fill us with peace as only you can do.

Isaiah 51:12; Jeremiah 29:11–13

AT NIGHT

I Will Bless Those Who Weep

"Blessed are you who are poor,
    for yours is the kingdom of God.
Blessed are you who hunger now,
    for you will be satisfied.
Blessed are you who weep now,
    for you will laugh.
Blessed are you when people hate you,
    when they exclude you and insult you
and reject your name as evil,
    because of the Son of Man.

"Rejoice in that day and leap for joy, because great is your reward in heaven."

Lord, you once said that the poor will always be with us. You could have said the same about the grieving because life has its seasons of loss. Be near to those among us who are grieving. Bring something good from our affliction. Number us among those you call "blessed."

Luke 6:20–23

Monday

IN THE MORNING

Though You Are in Darkness, I Will Be Your Light

But as for me, I watch in hope for the LORD,
    I wait for God my Savior;
    my God will hear me.
Do not gloat over me, my enemy!
    Though I have fallen, I will rise.
Though I sit in darkness,
    the LORD will be my light.

"There is hope for your future," declares the LORD.

"I am the light of the world. Whoever follows me will never walk in darkness, but will have the light of life."

Lord, in darkness, be my light. Remind me of your goodness. Help me to see the evidence of your strong love. When I reach out, may your hand guide me. Help me to remember that I am not alone, for you are always with me.

Micah 7:7–8; Jeremiah 31:17; John 8:12

AT NIGHT

I Will Not Disappoint You

My tears have been my food
    day and night,
while people say to me all day long,
    "Where is your God?"...
Why, my soul, are you downcast?
    Why so disturbed within me?
Put your hope in God,
    for I will yet praise him,
    my Savior and my God.

The Sovereign LORD will wipe away the tears
    from all faces;
he will remove the disgrace of his people
    from all the earth.

In that day they will say,
"Surely this is our God;
    we trusted in him, and he saved us.
This is the LORD, we trusted in him;
    let us rejoice and be glad in his salvation."

Lord, I can either trust myself or trust you. I can either conclude that I am the ultimate judge of reality or that you are. My feelings are so raw and real and yet I know I cannot rely on them. So one day, along with many others, I will surely say, "This is my God, I trusted in him, and he saved me."

Psalm 42:3, 5 (TNIV); Isaiah 25:8–9

Tuesday

IN THE MORNING

Believe in Me and You Will Live

On his arrival, Jesus found that Lazarus had already been in the tomb for four days. Now Bethany was less than two miles from Jerusalem, and many Jews had come to Martha and Mary to comfort them in the loss of their brother....

"Lord," Martha said to Jesus, "if you had been here, my brother would not have died. But I know that even now God will give you whatever you ask."

Jesus said to her, "Your brother will rise again."

Martha answered, "I know he will rise again in the resurrection at the last day."

Jesus said to her, "I am the resurrection and the life. Anyone who believes in me will live, even though they die; and whoever lives by believing in me will never die."

Lord Jesus, death had already dropped like a final, dreadful curtain over Lazarus, cutting him off from everyone he loved, including you. Yet it wasn't final; it never is for those who love you. Thank you not only for promising to resurrect us but for displaying your power to keep that promise.

John 11:17–26 (TNIV)

AT NIGHT

I Am Troubled by Your Sorrows

When Jesus saw her [Mary] weeping ... he was deeply moved in spirit and troubled. "Where have you laid him?" he asked.

"Come and see, Lord," they replied.

Jesus wept....

Jesus ... came to the tomb. It was a cave with a stone laid across the entrance. "Take away the stone," he said.

"But, Lord," said Martha, the sister of the dead man, "by this time there is a bad odor, for he has been there four days."

Then Jesus said, "Did I not tell you that if you believed, you will see the glory of God?"

So they took away the stone....

Jesus called in a loud voice, "Lazarus, come out!" The dead man came out, his hands and feet wrapped with strips of linen, and a cloth around his face.

Jesus said to them, "Take off the grave clothes and let him go."

Lord, you wept when your friend died, even though you knew you were going to raise him from the dead. Thank you for being a Savior who understands our grief and comprehends our sorrows. Never let me grieve as one who is without hope but as one who believes that you indeed are the resurrection and the life.

John 11:33–35, 38–41, 43–44 (TNIV)

Wednesday

IN THE MORNING

I Will Clothe You with Immortality

Listen, I tell you a mystery: We will not all sleep, but we will all be changed—in a flash, in the twinkling of an eye, at the last trumpet. For the trumpet will sound, the dead will be raised imperishable, and we will be changed. For the perishable must clothe itself with the imperishable, and the mortal with immortality. When the perishable has been clothed with the imperishable, and the mortal with immortality, then the saying that is written will come true: "Death has been swallowed up in victory."

"Where, O death, is your victory?
Where, O death, is your sting?"

Father, in a flash, in the twinkling of an eye, we will all be changed. When earthly hope is perishing, help me to hold onto the hope that comes from above, where you are, where I am heading. I pray this, now and forever, amen.

1 Corinthians 15:51–55

AT NIGHT

I Will Comfort You in Your Sufferings

Praise be to the God and Father of our Lord Jesus Christ, the Father of compassion and the God of all comfort, who comforts us in all our troubles, so that we can comfort those in any trouble with the comfort we ourselves have received from God. For just as the sufferings of Christ flow over into our lives, so also through Christ our comfort overflows. If we are distressed, it is for your comfort and salvation; if we are comforted, it is for your comfort, which produces in you patient endurance of the same sufferings we suffer. And our hope for you is firm, because we know that just as you share in our sufferings, so also you share in our comfort.

Lord, St. Paul linked his experience of your sufferings to his experience of your comfort. Remind me that, I, too, am part of your body, linked to you both in suffering and in comfort. Transform my troubles into something worthwhile. Comfort me so that I might comfort others.

2 Corinthians 1:3–7

Thursday

Thanksgiving Day
Nov. 27, 2014

IN THE MORNING

Joy Will Overtake Your Sorrow

Those who sow with tears
    will reap with songs of joy.
Those who go out weeping,
    carrying seed to sow,
will return with songs of joy,
    carrying sheaves with them.

The ransomed of the LORD will return.
    They will enter Zion with singing;
    everlasting joy will crown their heads.
Gladness and joy will overtake them,
    and sorrow and sighing will flee away.

Lord, I ask you to use the hard times to produce better times in my life. Help me to learn, to trust, and to grow — not despite but because of my difficulties. Chase away my sorrows and replace them with your joy. Renew my soul and glorify yourself through me.

Psalm 126:5–6 (TNIV); Isaiah 51:11

AT NIGHT

Your Body Can Rest in Hope

David said about him [Jesus]:

"I saw the Lord always before me.
　　Because he is at my right hand,
　　I will not be shaken.
Therefore my heart is glad and my tongue rejoices;
　　my body also will live in hope,
because you will not abandon me to the realm of the dead,
　　you will not let your Holy One see decay.
You have made known to me the paths of life;
　　you will fill me with joy in your presence."

Jesus, you are always with me, showing me how to live. Day after day you give me grace. Through hardship and darkness and every kind of difficulty you lead me. Even in death you will be there. My body will rest in hope, for you will raise me and fill me again with joy in your presence.

Acts 2:25–28

Friday

IN THE MORNING

I Will Be Like a Mother to You

As a mother comforts her child,
    so will I comfort you.

How often I have longed to gather your children together, as a hen gathers her chicks under her wings.

Therefore, this is what the LORD says: "I will return to Jerusalem with mercy, and there my house will be rebuilt. And the measuring line will be stretched out over Jerusalem," declares the LORD Almighty.

Proclaim further: This is what the LORD Almighty says: "My towns will again overflow with prosperity, and the LORD will again comfort Zion and choose Jerusalem."

Lord, be like a mother enfolding me in your all-forgiving arms. Help me to rest there, comforted at your breast. Make me to know your love once more.

Isaiah 66:13; Matthew 23:37; Zechariah 1:16–17

AT NIGHT

I Will Comfort You Again

Even when I am old and gray,
　　do not forsake me, O God,
till I declare your power to the next generation,
　　your might to all who are to come.
Your righteousness reaches to the skies, O God,
　　you who have done great things.
　　Who, O God, is like you?
Though you have made me see troubles, many and bitter,
　　you will restore my life again;
from the depths of the earth
　　you will again bring me up.
You will increase my honor
　　and comfort me once again.
I will praise you with the harp
　　for your faithfulness, O my God;
I will sing praise to you with the lyre,
　　O Holy One of Israel.

Lord, though I have seen troubles, many and bitter, you have never forsaken me. Thank you for staying power, for the buoyancy of hope, for the energy of life. Keep me strong until the end, I pray, and I will continue to sing your praises.

Psalm 71:18–22

Saturday

IN THE MORNING

The Hope I Give Will Not Disappoint You

We have this hope as an anchor for the soul, firm and secure.

Therefore, since we have been justified through faith, we have peace with God through our Lord Jesus Christ, through whom we have gained access by faith into this grace in which we now stand. And we rejoice in the hope of the glory of God. Not only so, but we also rejoice in our sufferings, because we know that suffering produces perseverance; perseverance, character; and character, hope. And hope does not disappoint us, because God has poured out his love into our hearts by the Holy Spirit, whom he has given us.

"The Root of Jesse will spring up,
　　one who will arise to rule over the nations;
the Gentiles will hope in him."

May the God of hope fill you with all joy and peace as you trust in him, so that you may overflow with hope by the power of the Holy Spirit.

Lord, despair and discouragement never come from you. How could they since you are the God of hope! Whatever happens, may this hope be an anchor for my soul, keeping me steady no matter the turbulence I face.

Hebrews 6:19; Romans 5:1–5; Romans 15:12–13

AT NIGHT

I Will Turn Your Mourning into Gladness

For the LORD will ransom Jacob
    and redeem them from the hand of those stronger
        than they.
They will come and shout for joy on the heights of Zion;
    they will rejoice in the bounty of the LORD—
the grain, the new wine and the oil,
    the young of the flocks and herds.
They will be like a well-watered garden,
    and they will sorrow no more.
Then maidens will dance and be glad,
    young men and old as well.
I will turn their mourning into gladness;
    I will give them comfort and joy instead of sorrow.
I will satisfy the priests with abundance,
    and my people will be filled with my bounty,"
                declares the LORD.

Father, I will rejoice in your goodness, believing that you will turn my mourning into gladness and my sorrow into comfort. Fill me, God, with your abundance. Let me taste of your kindness, my Lord and my God.

Jeremiah 31:11–14

I WILL REMEMBER THIS

"For I know the plans I have for you," declares the LORD, "plans to prosper you and not to harm you, plans to give you hope and a future. Then you will call upon me and come and pray to me, and I will listen to you. You will seek me and find me when you seek me with all your heart. I will be found by you," declares the LORD.

The Sovereign LORD will wipe away the tears
    from all faces;
he will remove the disgrace of his people
    from all the earth.

The LORD has spoken.

In that day they will say,
"Surely this is our God;
    we trusted in him, and he saved us.
This is the LORD, we trusted in him;
    let us rejoice and be glad in his salvation."

As a mother comforts her child,
    so will I comfort you.

Recently I finished Joan Didion's memoir, *The Year of Magical Thinking*, written after her husband's sudden death. Explaining why she decided to chronicle her first year without him, she says, "This is my attempt to make sense of the period that followed, weeks and then months that cut loose any fixed idea I

Jeremiah 29:11–14; Isaiah 25:8–9; Isaiah 66:13

had ever had about death, about illness, about probability and luck, about good fortune and bad, about marriage and children and memory, about grief, about the ways in which people do and do not deal with the fact that life ends, about the shallowness of sanity, about life itself."

The book is fascinating but darkly haunting, without hope. Relentlessly probing the questions such a death raises, she allows herself to wonder what her husband might have experienced: "'A moment of terror ... then an instant later the eternal dark?'" The final punctuation mark of her memoir is the starkest of all for she concludes that *no eye is on the sparrow.* It is a remark her husband once made to her, one that now summarizes her assessment of life.

Believing this, I am not sure how a person can go on. If in the scheme of things our suffering is a matter of "abiding indifference," as she says, how can one make sense of anything at all, let alone the death of a loved one? I suppose that an unflinching examination of death and the meaning of life on the part of an atheist could be interpreted as a mark of bravery, but what good is bravery in a world without meaning? What good is any kind of virtue in a world created entirely by chance?

Jesus held the opposite worldview. To believe in him is to stand with him on the side of hope. It is to affirm that individual human suffering is not a matter of cosmic indifference. It is to believe that a divine, all-loving eye is fixed on us even when we are insensible of God's gaze. That is the struggle of faith. It is the struggle Jesus faced on the cross.

If we stand with him in the midst of our questions and pain, then the final punctuation mark for our lives will one day affirm the truth of his words: "Are not five sparrows sold for two pennies? Yet not one of them is forgotten by God. Indeed, the very hairs of your head are all numbered. *Don't be afraid; you are worth more than many sparrows*" (Luke 12:6–7). With the prophet we will sing, "Surely this is our God; we trusted in him, and he saved us" (Isaiah 25:9).

12

God Speaks Words of Healing

יהוה רֹפֵא

YAHWEH ROPHE

The Hebrew word *rapa* means "to heal" or "to cure." Shortly after his people left Egypt, God revealed himself as *Yahweh Rophe*, "the LORD who heals." Though today we might point to germs or genetic disorders as the cause of many kinds of illnesses, the Bible goes deeper. It identifies sin as the root cause of every affliction we suffer because sin breaks our connection with the Creator and the perfect world he has made.

In the New Testament, the words *iaomai* and *therapeuo* mean "to heal, cure." The Gospels present Jesus Christ as the greatest of all physicians, curing souls as well as bodies. Jesus makes it clear that sickness does not always result from personal sin but also from living in a fallen world. His many miracles are a sign of the in-breaking kingdom of heaven.

LETTING THE WORD SHAPE ME

I'm a skeptic by nature. Yet the Bible is not at all cautious about linking faith with miracles, nor about inviting us to put our faith to work in healing prayer. So pray I do.

In fact, my prayer list is peppered with requests for healing. On my list currently is a young mother who days ago seemed close to death from a rare blood disorder, a toddler who has just undergone two-and-a-half hours of surgery for an infection that settled in his heart, and a friend who is battling a particularly aggressive form of cancer. Most of us know plenty of people in dire need of healing grace.

Several years ago I began praying for a friend of a friend diagnosed with fibromyalgia. Over the years she has expressed her thanks for prayer support with letters, email messages, and even an enormous pan of brownies. But I never had the pleasure of meeting her—until last week. One cold December night four praying friends and the woman herself spilled through my doorway. Together we shared a simple supper that seemed like a feast because of the joy we felt as we celebrated what God had done for her.

Later it occurred to me that such meetings must happen all the time in heaven—where people who have never met on earth embrace each other, thankful for how another's prayers have helped them.

The last few weeks have brought more good news. The young boy who underwent heart surgery is on the mend, and here's the latest on the woman who had been so critically ill:

She is walking without her walker and is talking well but slowly. Her MRI shows no damage in her brain. Life will not be "normal" for a while, but she is certainly on the right track now.

For a while, the news seemed good, too, for the friend battling cancer. But days ago it became clear that the cancer has returned. His wife wrote this note to all who had been praying: "We live a life of uncertainties, but serve an omniscient, loving God. That is our comfort."

It strikes me that she has struck the right balance, putting her faith not in an outcome but in a Person. I confess that I struggle with this balancing act. Instead of emphasizing God's love, I have tended to emphasize life's uncertainties. Even when someone I've prayed for recovers (which often happens), I find myself wondering whether prayer made the difference.

But perhaps uncertain is not a word that should characterize my prayers because over and over, Jesus spoke to his followers of the importance of having faith:

Daughter, your faith has healed you. Go in peace. (Luke 8:48)

I tell you the truth, if you have faith as small as a mustard seed, you can say to this mountain, "Move from here to there" and it will move. Nothing will be impossible for you. (Matthew 17:20)

Woman, you have great faith! Your request is granted. (Matthew 15:28)

So my prayer, at the end of this season of reading and praying through the healing words of God, is for a greater gift of faith. I want to have faith, not in a particular outcome but in the loving and powerful heart of Jesus, who spent most of his public ministry healing the sick, and driving out demons that tormented people. I want to pray in his name and with the faith he gives, growing daily into his likeness, so that I will one day hear from his lips: *Woman, you have great faith! Your request is granted.*

Sunday

IN THE MORNING

My Favor Lasts a Lifetime

I have heard your prayer and seen your tears; I will heal you.

I will exalt you, O LORD,
>for you lifted me out of the depths
>and did not let my enemies gloat over me.
O LORD my God, I called to you for help
>and you healed me.
O LORD, you brought me up from the grave;
>you spared me from going down into the pit.
Sing to the LORD, you saints of his;
>praise his holy name.
For his anger lasts only a moment,
>but his favor lasts a lifetime;
weeping may remain for a night,
>but rejoicing comes in the morning.

Lord, you have certainly heard my prayers and seen my tears. Answer me as you did Hezekiah, king of Judah, and I will rejoice in your healing grace.

2 Kings 20:5; Psalm 30:1–5

AT NIGHT

My Help Will Come to You

"Peace, peace, to those far and near,"
    says the LORD. "And I will heal them."

"Come, let us return to the LORD.
    He has torn us to pieces
    but he will heal us;
he has injured us
    but he will bind up our wounds.
After two days he will revive us;
    on the third day he will restore us,
    that we may live in his presence.
Let us acknowledge the LORD;
    let us press on to acknowledge him.
As surely as the sun rises,
    he will appear;
he will come to us like the winter rains,
    like the spring rains that water the earth."

Lord, I pray for "turning grace," for the power to turn away from sinful habits in order to turn toward you, my Creator and my healing God. Do not delay, but come to me like the winter rains, like the spring rains that water the earth. Heal me body and soul, I pray.

AMEN

Isaiah 57:19; Hosea 6:1–3

Monday

IN THE MORNING

I Will Hear from Heaven

If my people, who are called by my name, will humble them-selves and pray and seek my face and turn from their wicked ways, then will I hear from heaven and will forgive their sin and will heal their land.

There is a time for everything,
>   and a season for every activity under heaven:
>   a time to be born and a time to die,
>   a time to plant and a time to uproot,
>   a time to kill and a time to heal,
>   a time to tear down and a time to build,
>   a time to weep and a time to laugh,
>   a time to mourn and a time to dance.

Father, your word tells us there is a season for every activity under heaven. Please hear the cries of those who are in need of healing. Touch them with your power and inaugurate a season of healing in their lives. Restore them, bless them, and strengthen them, so that they may become the evidence of your mercy on earth.

2 Chronicles 7:14; Ecclesiastes 3:1–4

AT NIGHT

Then You Will Call, and I Will Answer

Is not this the kind of fasting I have chosen:
to loose the chains of injustice
    and untie the cords of the yoke,
to set the oppressed free
    and break every yoke?
Is it not to share your food with the hungry
    and to provide the poor wanderer with shelter—
when you see the naked, to clothe him,
    and not to turn away from your own flesh and blood?
Then your light will break forth like the dawn,
    and your healing will quickly appear;
then your righteousness will go before you,
    and the glory of the LORD will be your rear guard.
Then you will call, and the LORD will answer;
    you will cry for help, and he will say: Here am I.

Lord, forgive the anxiety and selfishness that mark my life, preventing me from being more generous to the needy. Let me pass on the good things you've given me, freely blessing others as you have blessed me.

Isaiah 58:6–9

Tuesday

IN THE MORNING

I Have Taken on Your Infirmities

I am the LORD, who heals you.

He was despised and rejected by others,
   a man of suffering, and familiar with pain.
Like one from whom people hide their faces
   he was despised, and we held him in low esteem.
Surely he took up our pain
   and bore our suffering
yet we considered him punished by God,
   stricken by him, and afflicted.
But he was pierced for our transgressions,
   he was crushed for our iniquities;
the punishment that brought us peace was on him,
   and by his wounds we are healed.
We all, like sheep, have gone astray,
   each of us has turned to our own way;
and the LORD has laid on him
   the iniquity of us all.

Lord, our sins were so grievous, our offences so serious, that there was no remedy capable of curing us — until you came. You have borne our sorrows and suffered our punishment. On you was the chastisement that made us whole. You are, indeed, the Lord who heals us!

Exodus 15:26; Isaiah 53:3–6 (TNIV)

AT NIGHT

Your Faith Can Make a Difference

A few days later, when Jesus again entered Capernaum, the people heard that he had come home. So many gathered that there was no room left, not even outside the door, and he preached the word to them. Some men came, bringing to him a paralytic, carried by four of them. Since they could not get him to Jesus because of the crowd, they made an opening in the roof above Jesus and, after digging through it, lowered the mat the paralyzed man was lying on. When Jesus saw their faith, he said to the paralytic, "Son, your sins are forgiven."

… He said to the paralytic, "I tell you, get up, take your mat and go home." He got up, took his mat and walked out in full view of them all. This amazed everyone and they praised God, saying, "We have never seen anything like this!"

Lord, increase my faith so that I can pray effectively for others. Let it overflow to those who are ill. May your power come down to heal and to give them peace, I pray.

Mark 2:1–5, 10–12

Wednesday

IN THE MORNING

Believe and You Will See

While Jesus was still speaking, someone came from the house of Jairus, the synagogue ruler. "Your daughter is dead," he said. "Don't bother the teacher any more."

Hearing this, Jesus said to Jairus, "Don't be afraid; just believe, and she will be healed."

When he arrived at the house of Jairus, he did not let anyone go in with him except Peter, John and James, and the child's father and mother. Meanwhile, all the people were wailing and mourning for her. "Stop wailing," Jesus said. "She is not dead but asleep."

They laughed at him, knowing that she was dead. But he took her by the hand and said, "My child, get up!" Her spirit returned, and at once she stood up.

Lord, when I or someone I love becomes ill, help me to look first to you. Protect me from fear, and give me your peace. Help me to pray with the power of your Spirit, believing that with your grace all things are possible.

Luke 8:49–55

AT NIGHT

Cry Out to Me in Your Trouble

Then they cried to the LORD in their trouble,
    and he saved them from their distress.
He sent forth his word and healed them;
    he rescued them from the grave.
Let them give thanks to the LORD for his unfailing love
    and his wonderful deeds for men.

Heal me, O LORD, and I will be healed;
    save me and I will be saved,
    for you are the one I praise.

*Lord, I bring the sick and the afflicted before you tonight, those I am
regularly praying for. I cry out on their behalf. Send forth your word
and your truth and heal them. Fill them with your unfailing love that
they may praise you for your wonderful deeds.*

Psalm 107:19–21; Jeremiah 17:14

Thursday

IN THE MORNING

I Reward Persistent Prayer

Jesus withdrew to the region of Tyre and Sidon. A Canaanite woman from that vicinity came to him, crying out, "Lord, Son of David, have mercy on me! My daughter is suffering terribly from demon-possession."

Jesus did not answer a word. So his disciples came to him and urged him, "Send her away, for she keeps crying out after us."

He answered, "I was sent only to the lost sheep of Israel."

The woman came and knelt before him. "Lord, help me!" she said.

He replied, "It is not right to take the children's bread and toss it to their dogs."

"Yes, Lord," she said, "but even the dogs eat the crumbs that fall from their masters' table."

Then Jesus answered, "Woman, you have great faith! Your request is granted." And her daughter was healed from that very hour.

Lord, thank you for the story of this woman who did not give up and did not take offense. Help me to persevere for those close to me who need your healing touch. Don't let me take offense if you don't answer me right away. But please, do not delay. Come with your healing power.

Matthew 15:21–28

AT NIGHT

You Only Need a Little Faith

When they came to the crowd, a man approached Jesus and knelt before him. "Lord, have mercy on my son," he said. "He has seizures and is suffering greatly. He often falls into the fire or into the water. I brought him to your disciples, but they could not heal him."

... Jesus rebuked the demon, and it came out of the boy, and he was healed from that moment.

Then the disciples came to Jesus in private and asked, "Why couldn't we drive it out?"

He replied, "Because you have so little faith. I tell you the truth, if you have faith as small as a mustard seed, you can say to this mountain, 'Move from here to there' and it will move. Nothing will be impossible for you."

Lord, give me the kind of faith that is able to move mountains, the kind that is not intimidated by circumstances nor limited by imagination. Strengthen me so that guided by your Spirit, I will know that nothing is impossible for you to do through me.

Matthew 17:14–20

Friday

IN THE MORNING

I Am Stronger Than Any Evil You Face

For you who revere my name, the sun of righteousness will rise with healing in its wings.

Jesus withdrew with his disciples to the lake, and a large crowd from Galilee followed. When they heard all he was doing, many people came to him from Judea, Jerusalem, Idumea, and the regions across the Jordan and around Tyre and Sidon. Because of the crowd he told his disciples to have a small boat ready for him, to keep the people from crowding him. For he had healed many, so that those with diseases were pushing forward to touch him. Whenever the evil spirits saw him, they fell down before him and cried out, "You are the Son of God."

Lord, no wonder the crowds swarmed around you, each person hoping to get near enough to touch you. Thank you that your power is greater than our disease. Shelter me now beneath your healing wings.

Malachi 4:2; Mark 3:7–11

AT NIGHT

I Want to Use You

I will heal their waywardness
and love them freely.

Jesus went through all the towns and villages, teaching in their synagogues, preaching the good news of the kingdom and healing every disease and sickness. When he saw the crowds, he had compassion on them, because they were harassed and helpless, like sheep without a shepherd. Then he said to his disciples, "The harvest is plentiful but the workers are few. Ask the Lord of the harvest, therefore, to send out workers into his harvest field."

He called his twelve disciples to him and gave them authority to drive out evil spirits and to heal every disease and sickness.

Lord, your intentions are to heal and to restore, to turn the hearts of the people away from darkness and toward the light. May I be a light and a healer in my own place. Make me a blessing to others.

Hosea 14:4; Matthew 9:35 – 10:1

Saturday

IN THE MORNING

Pray for Each Other

Is anyone among you in trouble? Let them pray. Is anyone happy? Let them sing songs of praise. Is anyone among you sick? Let them call the elders of the church to pray over them and anoint them with oil in the name of the Lord. And the prayer offered in faith will make them well; the Lord will raise them up. If they have sinned, they will be forgiven. Therefore confess your sins to each other and pray for each other so that you may be healed. The prayer of a righteous person is powerful and effective.

Lord, please restore prayer in your church throughout the world. Help us to be honest about our failings, to pray regularly together, to worship you in spirit and in truth, and to pray for those who are ill. Heal us and help us — and remind us that we are your body here on earth.

James 5:13–16 (TNIV)

AT NIGHT

There Will Be No More Night

He heals the brokenhearted
  and binds up their wounds.

Then the angel showed me the river of the water of life, as clear as crystal, flowing from the throne of God and of the Lamb down the middle of the great street of the city. On each side of the river stood the tree of life, bearing twelve crops of fruit, yielding its fruit every month. And the leaves of the tree are for the healing of the nations. No longer will there be any curse. The throne of God and of the Lamb will be in the city, and his servants will serve him. They will see his face, and his name will be on their foreheads. There will be no more night. They will not need the light of a lamp or the light of the sun, for the Lord God will give them light. And they will reign for ever and ever.

Lord, thank you for the assurance that in the end all will be well for those who belong to you. No longer will there be any curse — no affliction, suffering, or death. For we will see you face to face and you will be our light forever.

Psalm 147:3; Revelation 22:1 – 5

I WILL REMEMBER THIS

Heal me, O LORD, and I will be healed;
    save me and I will be saved,
      for you are the one I praise.

Daughter, your faith has healed you. Go in peace.

The prayer of a righteous person is powerful and effective.

Many years ago I attended a women's breakfast in a college town in Ohio. That day one of the women told an unusual story. I don't remember the details but the core of the story was unforgettable. It seems she had been suffering from back pain for some time. Her condition was so severe that she couldn't even walk without bending over. One day, her four-year-old daughter wondered out loud "when mama was going to have another baby." Knowing how difficult it would be to sustain a pregnancy in her condition, the mother replied: "Honey, Momma and Daddy would really like to have another baby, but God would have to heal my back before it would be safe for me to have one. We just can't right now."

Some time later, she and her family were vacationing at the ocean. So debilitating was her pain that her husband had to carry her into the water whenever she wanted to swim. One day when she had just entered the surf an enormous wave broke

Jeremiah 17:14; Luke 8:48; James 5:16

over her, sending her somersaulting through the water. As soon as she regained her footing she realized something in her body had changed. In fact she was standing straight up without any pain. Oddly, her first thought was not, "My back is healed!" Instead, the words that came into her mind were these: "I must be pregnant!" And indeed she was. A visit to the doctor's office subsequently confirmed that she was going to have another child. Apparently God is not only a great physician but a pretty good chiropractor as well!

But what about all the people who don't receive a healing? On any given day thousands, perhaps millions, of people are storming heaven for a miracle, but no miracle is forthcoming. Why some are healed while others are not is a mystery no one can solve, though perhaps the passage from James, linking righteousness and power, identifies one key factor.

Regardless of how God answers our prayers, I believe that he sometimes does use our bodies to display his redemptive work. When that happens, we become signs of his in-breaking kingdom, attesting to the hope we have in Christ that someday we and all of creation will be exactly what he intends us to be — healthy, whole and at peace. Until then, let us ask God to help us become the kind of people who can pray with power, full of faith and hope.

13

Jesus—the Last, Most Tender Word

יְשׁוּעַ

YESHUA

There is tenderness even in the name "Jesus," a name that contains a promise. Rendered *Yeshua* in Hebrew, it means "Yahweh is salvation," thereby linking Jesus to the holiest name for God in Scripture. God comes into clearest focus in the life of Jesus—a God who surprises us not only by his power but by the greatness of his love. Jesus is also called the *Logos* or "Word." He is God's definitive message to the human race.

LETTING THE WORD SHAPE ME

Years ago I had the opportunity of spending a little time with Malcolm Muggeridge, a famous British journalist, known for his acerbic wit. Though I was looking forward to meeting him, I also felt a bit intimidated. I wondered whether during the course of our time together I might say something awkward or stupid, something that would inevitably attract his skewering wit. But when the time came, I felt completely at ease. In fact, my meeting with him was one of the most memorable of my life, though I don't recall what we talked about. What I will never forget, however, is the kindness with which he treated me, as though I were the single, most important person on the planet.

I expect Muggeridge had that effect on a lot of people. But why was my experience of him so different from his public persona? Surely a large part of the difference might be explained by his growing faith. Though he had once dismissed Christianity as a "load of rubbish," he had later embraced it. Perhaps also this man, who was famous for his acid wit, reserved his sharpest barbs for people who needed them, people in the public eye who were advocating policies that he saw as damaging or dangerous to others.

When I began searching the Gospels for the tender words of Jesus, I remembered my encounter with Muggeridge. And that memory triggered another. A friend had recently asked an intriguing question: "If Jesus is God and God is love, why does Jesus sometimes seem not very nice in the Gospels?" It was a question I had asked myself more than once. Among other things, my friend may have been thinking about some of the things Jesus said, words that sounded anything but tender:

Woe to you, because you are like unmarked graves, which men walk over without knowing it.

You snakes! You brood of vipers! How will you escape being condemned to hell?

You are like whitewashed tombs, which look beautiful on the outside but on the inside are full of dead men's bones and everything unclean.

You belong to your father, the devil, and you want to carry out your father's desire. He was a murderer from the beginning.

Perhaps part of the answer to my friend's question is that love is not always "nice," especially in the face of wickedness.

As I continued reading through Jesus' words in the Gospels, I was also reminded of how undiplomatic he could be. So often, when faced with the opportunity to say a word that would calm tensions and subdue tempers, Jesus said something that inflamed the situation, as though poking a stick into a beehive.

It strikes me that Jesus' harshest words, like Muggeridge's, were directed at people who needed skewering—the religious leaders of his day who resisted the gospel and tried to influence ordinary people against him. To be tender toward such men would be to turn his back on those he had come to save. It would be like looking on while someone held another person's head under water, depriving him of life.

So often, Jesus' words are as startling as they are challenging. As I read through a red-letter version of the Gospels searching for his tender words, I found many other words that upset my comfortable Christian applecart, words like these:

You have heard that it was said, "Eye for eye, and tooth for tooth." But I tell you, Do not resist an evil person. If someone strikes you on the right cheek, turn to him the other also.

It has been said, "Anyone who divorces his wife must give her a certificate of divorce." But I tell you that anyone who divorces his wife, except for marital unfaithfulness, causes her to become an adulteress, and anyone who marries the divorced woman commits adultery."

How, I wondered, could such words possibly be construed as tender? The more I read, the more I began to realize that experiencing the tenderness of Jesus is often a matter of perspective. For instance, the passage exhorting us to love our enemies can seem like an impossible command. But it also reveals the heart of Christ himself, who when we were yet his enemies, treated us with the kind of extreme love that he commends to his followers.

But what about the passage concerning divorce? It would certainly have sounded harsh in the ears of a Jewish male. But to the ears of a Jewish woman, the words would have sounded sweet, because at that time a husband could divorce his wife for just about any reason, including a burnt dinner! As usual, Jesus was taking the side of the weak, of those who had no one to protect them.

Fortunately, my search through the Gospels uncovered many straightforwardly tender words. Over and over I saw the incontrovertible evidence of his kindness—to the sick, the weary, the outcast, the hungry, the poor, and the demon-possessed. To anyone willing, he spoke words of encouragement and love. He was God walking in the creation he loved, touching, restoring, healing, and imparting hope.

Even his actions and miracles are "words" to us, communicating God's profound love, telling us of his intention to restore and redeem us. The more I listen to the tender words of Jesus, identifying myself with the needy, the more I find myself relaxing, calming down, leaning into the words he speaks to reshape my soul:

Come to me, all you who are weary and burdened, and I will give you rest.

Don't be afraid, you are worth more than many sparrows.

My yoke is easy and my burden is light.

Friend, your sins are forgiven.

Remain in my love.

Sunday

IN THE MORNING

I Am the Word

In the beginning was the Word, and the Word was with God, and the Word was God. He was with God in the beginning.

Through him all things were made; without him nothing was made that has been made. In him was life, and that life was the light of men. The light shines in the darkness, but the darkness has not understood it....

The Word became flesh and made his dwelling among us. We have seen his glory, the glory of the One and Only, who came from the Father, full of grace and truth.

"The virgin will be with child and will give birth to a son, and they will call him Immanuel"—which means, "God with us."

Lord, speak your all-powerful words into my heart. Let me be filled with your Word as with light. Help me to see you as you are, King of kings and Lord of lords, Wonderful Counselor, Prince of Peace—the Mighty God come to dwell with his people.

John 1:1–5, 14; Matthew 1:23

AT NIGHT

I Did Not Come to Condemn You

An angel of the Lord appeared to him in a dream and said, "Joseph son of David, do not be afraid to take Mary home as your wife, because what is conceived in her is from the Holy Spirit. She will give birth to a son, and you are to give him the name Jesus, because he will save his people from their sins."

For God so loved the world that he gave his one and only Son, that whoever believes in him shall not perish but have eternal life. For God did not send his Son into the world to condemn the world, but to save the world through him.

Two other men, both criminals, were also led out with him to be executed. When they came to the place called the Skull, there they crucified him, along with the criminals — one on his right, the other on his left. Jesus said, "Father, forgive them, for they do not know what they are doing."

Jesus, you are the expression of God's love, the incarnation of his mercy. You are courageous and kind, forgiving and good. You had every reason to condemn, but instead you forgave. Mercy and more mercy — this is the tender word you have always spoken to me.

Matthew 1:20–21; John 3:16–17; Luke 23:32–34

Monday

IN THE MORNING

I Call You "Friend"

"Friend, your sins are forgiven."

Then Peter came to Jesus and asked, "Lord, how many times shall I forgive my brother when he sins against me? Up to seven times?"

Jesus answered, "I tell you, not seven times, but seventy-seven times."

Thank you, Jesus, for calling me "friend." As your Word says, "A friend loves at all times, and a brother is born for adversity." You, my Brother, have loved me well. The next time someone offends me, help me to remember who I am—your friend—called to forgive even as I have been forgiven.

Luke 5:20; Matthew 18:21–22

AT NIGHT

I Set You Free

"The Spirit of the Lord is on me,
   because he has anointed me
   to preach good news to the poor.
He has sent me to proclaim freedom for the prisoners
   and recovery of sight for the blind,
to release the oppressed,
   to proclaim the year of the Lord's favor."

Then he [Jesus] rolled up the scroll, gave it back to the attendant and sat down. The eyes of everyone in the synagogue were fastened on him, and he began by saying to them, "Today this scripture is fulfilled in your hearing."

Lord, you are the yes to all of God's promises. You give sight to the blind, open up prison doors, and proclaim a year of goodness and favor. Lord, seek out the lowly, search out the oppressed, let your favor be proclaimed throughout the world.

Luke 4:18–21

Tuesday

IN THE MORNING

I Will Never Drive You Away

Then Jesus declared, "I am the bread of life. Whoever comes to me will never go hungry, and whoever believes in me will never be thirsty. But as I told you, you have seen me and still you do not believe. All that the Father gives me will come to me, and whoever comes to me I will never drive away. For I have come down from heaven not to do my will but to do the will of him who sent me. And this is the will of him who sent me, that I shall lose none of all those he has given me, but raise them up at the last day. For my Father's will is that everyone who looks to the Son and believes in him shall have eternal life, and I will raise them up at the last day."

Lord, thank you for promising never to drive me away. I want to hold onto that promise, to believe it so firmly, that even at the moment of my death, when it seems as though I am being driven away, I will not doubt your promise. Hold me fast and keep me with you always.

John 6:35–40 (TNIV)

AT NIGHT

Feed on Me

"Whoever eats my flesh and drinks my blood has eternal life, and I will raise them up at the last day. For my flesh is real food and my blood is real drink. Whoever eats my flesh and drinks my blood remains in me, and I in them. Just as the living Father sent me and I live because of the Father, so the one who feeds on me will live because of me. This is the bread that came down from heaven. Your ancestors ate manna and died, but whoever feeds on this bread will live forever."

Lord, I want to feed on you, to be nourished by your body and your blood, to be strengthened and transformed by your incarnation and your sacrifice. Help me to remain in you. Raise me up to live forever.

John 6:54–58 (TNIV)

Wednesday

IN THE MORNING

Stop Worrying!

Then Jesus said to his disciples: "Therefore I tell you, do not worry about your life, what you will eat; or about your body, what you will wear. Life is more than food, and the body more than clothes. Consider the ravens: They do not sow or reap, they have no storeroom or barn; yet God feeds them. And how much more valuable you are than birds!"

Lord, forgive me for all the wasted, anxious moments of my life. Help me today to take your Word literally—to stop worrying! Teach me to live more simply by focusing on doing your will and then leaving the rest to you, I pray.

Luke 12:22–24

AT NIGHT

I Loved You When You Were Far From Me

"You have heard that it was said, 'Love your neighbor and hate your enemy.' But I tell you: Love your enemies and pray for those who persecute you, that you may be children of your Father in heaven. He causes his sun to rise on the evil and the good, and sends rain on the righteous and the unrighteous. If you love those who love you, what reward will you get? Are not even the tax collectors doing that? And if you greet only your own people, what are you doing more than others? Do not even pagans do that? Be perfect, therefore, as your heavenly Father is perfect."

Lord, passages like this reveal your heart to the world. You are a God whose love encompasses even your enemies. And once I was your enemy. Help me to remember this and to reflect your goodness the next time someone offends me. Change, me, Lord, through the power of your love.

Matthew 5:43–48 (TNIV)

Thursday

IN THE MORNING

I Am the Good Shepherd

He tends his flock like a shepherd:
>He gathers the lambs in his arms
and carries them close to his heart.

"I am the good shepherd. The good shepherd lays down his life for the sheep. The hired hand is not the shepherd who owns the sheep. So when he sees the wolf coming, he abandons the sheep and runs away....

"I am the good shepherd; I know my sheep and my sheep know me — just as the Father knows me and I know the Father — and I lay down my life for the sheep. I have other sheep that are not of this sheep pen. I must bring them also. They too will listen to my voice, and there shall be one flock and one shepherd."

Jesus, thank you for giving your life not grudgingly but willingly, for protecting me with your rod and your staff, for keeping me safe and carrying me close to your heart. Thank you for laying down your life so that I might have life.

Isaiah 40:11; John 10:11–16

AT NIGHT

Remain in My Love

"As the Father has loved me, so have I loved you. Now remain in my love. If you keep my commands, you will remain in my love, just as I have kept my Father's commands and remain in his love. I have told you this so that my joy may be in you and that your joy may be complete. My command is this: Love each other as I have loved you. Greater love has no one than this, to lay down one's life for one's friends. You are my friends if you do what I command. I no longer call you servants, because servants do not know their master's business. Instead, I have called you friends, for everything that I learned from my Father I have made known to you."

Lord, I want always to be your friend. Thank you that the love you speak of doesn't depend on whether I'm attractive, smart, perfect, or clever. Let my one purpose in life be to bring you joy and to express my love by obeying your commands.

John 15:9–15 (TNIV)

Friday

IN THE MORNING

I Pray for You

"I will remain in the world no longer, but they are still in the world, and I am coming to you. Holy Father, protect them by the power of your name—the name you gave me—so that they may be one as we are one. While I was with them, I protected them and kept them safe by that name you gave me."

"My prayer is not for them alone. I pray also for those who will believe in me through their message, that all of them may be one, Father, just as you are in me and I am in you. . . .

"Father, I want those you have given me to be with me where I am, and to see my glory, the glory you have given me because you loved me before the creation of the world."

Because Jesus lives forever, he has a permanent priesthood. Therefore he is able to save completely those who come to God through him, because he always lives to intercede for them.

Father, thank you for hearing the prayer of your Son and for protecting the souls of all who believe in him. Please be at work among believers, bringing us to a deep repentance for the ways we have worked against each other. Heal our divisions. Make us humble. Bring us together for the purpose of glorifying your name, amen.

John 17:11–12; John 17:20–24; Hebrews 7:24–25

AT NIGHT

I Call the Weary to Come to Me

"Come to me, all you who are weary and burdened, and I will give you rest. Take my yoke upon you and learn from me, for I am gentle and humble in heart, and you will find rest for your souls. For my yoke is easy and my burden is light."

"Do not let your hearts be troubled. Trust in God; trust also in me. In my Father's house are many rooms; if it were not so, I would have told you. I am going there to prepare a place for you. And if I go and prepare a place for you, I will come back and take you to be with me that you also may be where I am."

Lord, help me to let go of the burdens I carry that are not from you. Increase my trust so that I can lay them down and then find rest for my soul. Let me be yoked to you, so that my burden, indeed, may be light.

Matthew 11:28–30; John 14:1–3

Saturday

IN THE MORNING

I Won't Send You Away Hungry

Jesus left there and went along the Sea of Galilee. Then he went up on a mountainside and sat down. Great crowds came to him, bringing the lame, the blind, the crippled, the mute and many others, and laid them at his feet; and he healed them. The people were amazed when they saw the mute speaking, the crippled made well, the lame walking and the blind seeing. And they praised the God of Israel.

Jesus called his disciples to him and said, "I have compassion for these people; they have already been with me three days and have nothing to eat. I do not want to send them away hungry, or they may collapse on the way."

Jesus Christ is the same yesterday and today and forever.

Jesus, you know what it's like to be human, to experience hunger and sickness and weakness. Thank you for your compassion, for using your power to feed, to heal, and to free us. No wonder the people flocked to you—a mighty God who lifts up the lowly!

Matthew 15:29–32; Hebrews 13:8

AT NIGHT

I Am Hungry

"For I was hungry and you gave me something to eat, I was thirsty and you gave me something to drink, I was a stranger and you invited me in, I needed clothes and you clothed me, I was sick and you looked after me, I was in prison and you came to visit me."

Then the righteous will answer him, "Lord, when did we see you hungry and feed you, or thirsty and give you something to drink? When did we see you a stranger and invite you in, or needing clothes and clothe you? When did we see you sick or in prison and go to visit you?"

The King will reply, "I tell you the truth, whatever you did for one of the least of these brothers and sisters of mine, you did for me."

Lord, you dwell with the lowly, the poor, and the weak of this world. Help me to do the same. Make me generous in the work of feeding and clothing and welcoming the needy, realizing that I am doing all these things for you.

Matthew 25:35–40 (TNIV)

I WILL REMEMBER THIS

God did not send his Son into the world to condemn the world, but to save the world through him.

Come to me, all you who are weary and burdened, and I will give you rest. Take my yoke upon you and learn from me, for I am gentle and humble in heart, and you will find rest for your souls. For my yoke is easy and my burden is light.

Do not let your hearts be troubled. Trust in God; trust also in me.

There is no more tender word from God than the Word made flesh. When God gave us Jesus, he gave us everything. Our confusion about who God is and how he thinks of us begins to fade as we focus on the life, death, and resurrection of Jesus Christ. If you are ever tempted to conclude that there is any meanness in God, any coldness or indifference toward you or anyone else on earth, you have only to look at the life of Jesus. His actions, his miracles, his words—everything about him communicates a God who is love. And it is God's generous, consistent love that is, of course, the message of this book.

The idea for the book came to me three years ago, shortly after I had experienced a particularly bruising wound to my faith. I knew I needed something to remind me that God still cared for me, so I decided to develop "a remedial course," one

John 3:17; Matthew 11:28–30; John 14:1

that would be drawn from the Scriptures themselves. It seems to me now that these months of soaking in the Bible's most encouraging words has been God's way of healing that wound and others, some of them afflicted through my own fault. But it has not been so much about assigning fault as it has been about assigning grace.

Focusing on his tender words has, for me, been something like melting the glaze off a car windshield after a brutal ice storm. I can see more clearly and move ahead more confidently, without the distorting ice.

I am still aware of my weakness, perhaps more than before. But I hope it has moved off center stage, a place that should be reserved for God alone.

Of course God remains a mystery, ever resistant to my attempts to define him by my own self-perceptions. His goodness does not shift because my understanding is clouded. His love does not wane based on my feelings. His faithfulness is not challenged because he does not act as I want him to or think he should.

I am reminded also that there is nothing sentimental or saccharine about God's tender words. As all his words, they are powerful, able to cut away whatever obscures our vision and keeps us from him. If we listen, his words will become the foundation on which our future is built and the rock on which we stand. They will shape our lives and spill over into the lives of many others.

May we listen.

Reference Sources

Page 42: Jonathan Saltzman, "'I Still Forgive Him,'" *The Boston Globe* (April 14, 2006).

Page 43: Lyndon Harris, in an interview for the documentary film *The Power of Forgiveness*, posted on Journey Films' website, *www.journeyfilms.com/content.asp?contentid=795*, accessed May 30, 2008.

Page 63: Robert Frost, "Mending Wall," *North of Boston* (New York: H. Holt, 1915).

Page 64: William D. Mounce, general editor, *Mounce's Complete Expository Dictionary of Old and New Testament Words* (Grand Rapids: Zondervan, 2006), 281.

Page 86: See James Bryan Smith with Lynda Graybeal, *A Spiritual Formation Workbook* (San Francisco: HarperSanFrancisco, 1991, 1993), 100.

Page 131: Father Richard Veras, "The Samaritan Woman and Pontius Pilate," *Magnificat* (March 2007), 138.

Page 152: "God's Provision," posted on *Teaching Art and Spiritual Walking*, November 11, 2005, www.homeschoolblogger.com/sjeffus/. Accessed May 30, 2008.

Page 173: Jerry Sittser, *The Will of God as a Way of Life* (Grand Rapids: Zondervan, 2000, 2004), 22–26.

Page 174: Ibid., 33.

Page 175: Ibid., 34–35 (italics in original).

Page 195: Jim Cymbala, *The Life God Blesses* (Grand Rapids: Zondervan, 2001), 144, 146.

Page 212: Since our conversation, Mark published the book under the title *The Holy Wild: Trusting in the Character of God* (Sisters, Ore.: Multnomah, 2003).

Page 235: Joan Didion, *The Year of Magical Thinking* (New York: Knopf, 2005), 7.

Praying the Names of God

A Daily Guide

Ann Spangler,
Bestselling Author of Women of the Bible

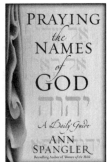

A twenty-six-week devotional study by the best-selling coauthor of *Women of the Bible*

Names in the ancient world did more than simply distinguish one person from another, they often conveyed the essential nature and character of a person. This is especially true when it comes to the names of God recorded in the Bible. *Praying the Names of God* explores the primary names and titles of God in the Old Testament to reveal the deeper meanings behind them.

El Shadday, Elohim, Adonay, Abba, El Elyon — God Almighty, Mighty Creator, Lord, Father, God Most High — these are just a few of the names and titles of God that yield rich insights into his nature and character. *Praying the Names of God* shows readers how to study and pray God's names by focusing each week on one of the primary names or titles of God.

- Monday — readers study a portion of Scripture that reveals the name.
- Tuesday — Thursday—readers pray specific Scripture passages related to the name.
- Friday — readers pray Scripture promises connected to the name.

By incorporating the divine names and titles into their prayers — and learning about the biblical context in which the name was revealed — readers will gain a more intimate understanding of who God is and how he can be relied on in every circumstance of their lives.

Praying the Names of God is a unique devotional, one that offers a rich program of daily prayer and study designed to lead people into fresh encounters with the living God.

Hardcover, Jacketed 978-0-310-25353-2

Praying the Names of Jesus

A Daily Guide

Ann Spangler,
Bestselling Author of
Praying the Names of God

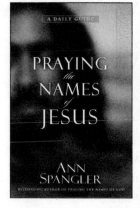

Joy, peace, and power—these are only some
of the gifts promised to those who trust in
the name of the Lord. Praying the Names of Jesus will lead readers
into a richer and more rewarding relationship with Christ by helping
them to understand and to pray his names on a daily basis. They will
also begin to see how each of his names holds within it a promise:
to be our Teacher, Healer, Friend, and Lord—to be God-with-Us no
matter the circumstances. Each week provides a unique devotional
program designed for personal prayer and study or for use in small
groups. In ways both surprising and profound this book reveals a rich
portrait of Jesus that will move readers toward a deeper experience
of his love and mercy.

Hardcover, Jacketed: 0-310-25345-4

Women of the Bible

A One-Year Devotional Study of Women in Scripture

Ann Spangler and
Jean E. Syswerda

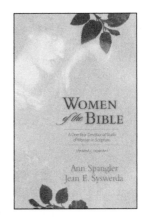

Women of the Bible focuses on fifty-two re-markable women in Scripture—women whose struggles to live with faith and courage are not unlike your own. And now this bestselling de-votional study book has been updated and expanded to enhance its flexibility, usefulness, and relevance for both individuals and groups.

Small groups will especially welcome the way the Bible studies have been streamlined to fit the unique needs of the group setting. Other important changes include:

- A list of all the women of the Bible keyed to Scripture
- A timeline of the foremost women of the Bible
- A list of women in Jesus' family tree
- A list of women in Jesus' life and ministry

Vital and deeply human, the women in this book encourage you through their failures as well as their successes. You'll see how God acted in surprising and wonderful ways to draw them—and you—to him-self. This year-long devotional offers a unique method to help you slow down and savor the story of God's unrelenting love for his people, of-fering a fresh perspective that will nourish and strengthen your per-sonal communion with him.

Hardcover, Jacketed 978-0-310-27055-3

Pick up a copy today at your favorite bookstore!

Mothers of the Bible

A Devotional

*Ann Spangler and
Jean E. Syswerda*

Children need the love, wisdom, and nurture that mothers are uniquely capable of giving. *Mothers of the Bible* can help you fulfill your own calling as a mother by offering insights from God's Word. Exploring the lives of women in the Bible can help strengthen your faith and your effectiveness as a mother. Like you, these mothers wanted the best for their children. And like you, they sometimes faced difficulties that challenged their faith. Looking to them can help deepen your understanding of Scripture, enabling you to experience more of God's love so you can reflect that love to your children.

Adapted from *Women of the Bible*, *Mothers of the Bible* furnishes a unique twelve-week devotional experience. Each week becomes a personal retreat focused on the life of a particular biblical mother.

Designed for personal prayer and study or for use in small groups, *Mothers of the Bible* will help you ground your relationship with your children on God's Word.

Hardcover, Printed 978-0-310-27239-7

Pick up a copy today at your favorite bookstore!

Women of the Bible

52 Stories for Prayer and Reflection

Ann Spangler

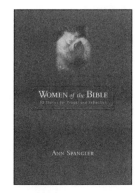

Though we are familiar with the Bible's most noteworthy men, many of us know little about women of the Bible and the important roles they played in the story of salvation.

The cast is long and colorful, including a parade of prostitutes, evil queens, peasants, and prophetesses. And though our culture differs vastly from theirs, we instinctively understand these women as they agonize over infertility, worry about their children, long for a little real affection, and struggle to find faith. Far from being one-dimensional characters, these are flesh-and-blood women whose mistakes and failings often mirror our own and whose collective wisdom yields rich insight into our struggle to live with faith and courage.

Taken from the bestseller *Women of the Bible*, each of the fifty-two stories in this book concludes with a brief reflection encouraging us to pray in light of the woman's story, thereby deepening our understanding of Scripture and our experience of prayer.

Hardcover, Printed 978-0-310-24493-6

Pick up a copy today at your favorite bookstore!

For more information on Ann Spangler,
please check out:
http://annspangler.com

Share Your Thoughts

With the Author: Your comments will be forwarded to
the author when you send them to *zauthor@zondervan.com*.

With Zondervan: Submit your review of this book
by writing to *zreview@zondervan.com*.

Free Online Resources at
www.zondervan.com/hello

 Zondervan AuthorTracker: Be notified whenever your
favorite authors publish new books, go on tour, or post
an update about what's happening in their lives.

 Daily Bible Verses and Devotions: Enrich your life
with daily Bible verses or devotions that help you start
every morning focused on God.

 Free Email Publications: Sign up for newsletters on
fiction, Christian living, church ministry, parenting, and
more.

 Zondervan Bible Search: Find and compare
Bible passages in a variety of translations at
www.zondervanbiblesearch.com.

 Other Benefits: Register yourself to receive online
benefits like coupons and special offers, or to participate
in research.